DISCOVERING
Motherhood

An Extraordinary Journey
through Everyday Life

BY ANNEMARIE SCOBEY

Ambassador Books, Inc.
Worcester • Massachusetts

Library of Congress Cataloging-in-Publication Data

Scobey, Annemarie, 1968-
  Discovering motherhood : an extraordinary journey through ordinary life / by Annemarie Scobey.
     p. cm.
  ISBN 1-929039-36-0 (pbk.)
  1. Motherhood. 2. Parenting. 3. Spiritual life. I. Title.

  HQ759.S297 2006
  306.874'3--dc22
                                          2006021159

ISBN-10: 1-929039-36-0
ISBN-13: 978-1-929039-36-4

Published in the United States by Ambassador Books, Inc.
91 Prescott Street, Worcester, Massachusetts 01605
(800) 577-0909

Printed in the United States of America.

For current information about all titles from Ambassador Books, Inc., visit our website at: www.ambassadorbooks.com.

Dedication

To Marianne and Paul Scobey,
my mom and dad,
with gratitude for teaching me
what family is — what love is

TABLE OF CONTENTS

Part I: Out of the Womb and into Our Lives - 7

Part II: Racing through Early Childhood - 37

Part III: We Feed Them and They Just Keep Growing - 105

PART I:

Out of the Womb and into Our Lives

CHAPTER ONE

Another Baby

*B*aby number two. Second child. Having another one. These phrases, tossed around with great frequency just a few months ago, when I was pregnant with my second baby, scared me a little. They all seemed to imply that I was doing something again. Something I had done before. And in the midst of disappointingly familiar morning sickness and swollen ankles, I wondered if having a second baby would simply be a repeat of having the first, except without the overwhelming awe that accompanied each new milestone. Looking back on the babyhood of my first child, Jacob, it seemed to be a string of wonderful accomplishments. Though the childcare books had taught me that the average infant rolls over at four months and sits at five, there was nothing average about my feelings when my own son did these things. He was a genius for discovering he had fingers, an athlete for being able to stand. As he bridged the gap from babyhood to life as a toddler, his feats became more complex, and I marveled in his newfound language skills.

As I entered the final trimester of pregnancy, Jacob was three and a half, and I was his biggest fan as he raced through little boyhood, learning to kick a soccer ball, jump off the porch, and spell his name. I watched him, though, with one hand on my ever-growing belly, wondering if I'd be able to tear my eyes from his race long enough to appreciate this new baby, who was still in the starting blocks. I didn't doubt that I'd love the baby, but I wasn't sure if I could love him with the passion and the unbridled excitement with which I loved Jacob.

I approached my due date warily, remembering all that a newborn demands. With Jacob, the late night feedings, the never-ending diaper changes, and the bouts of crying were buoyed by the thrill of every new accomplishment. I hoped I would rediscover the magic of those tiny milestones from so long ago, but feared that they might not hold the same excitement, the same suspense. I never watched reruns on TV because I didn't see the point of watching when you already knew the ending. I feared baby two would be a rerun.

Liam entered the world late one night, oblivious to all of my questions. Nursing on my breast minutes after being delivered, he assumed he would be loved and kept warm, and as I stroked his tiny cheek, some part of me emerged that had never before given birth, had never nursed, had never held a newborn. I was in awe. Again.

In the days and weeks that have followed Liam's birth, however, I am discovering that my awe is different the second time around. With Jacob, I had waited eagerly for each new developmental feat, each new sign of growth. I loved monthly doctor's appointments because I could see him getting longer and gaining weight. I grinned at him until my face hurt in an effort to coax out a first smile. But with Liam I know what is to come, and I don't feel the need to rush things. I love the smallness of him, the softness of his legs, the sheer newbornly feel of his head. When the doctor announced at his six-week check-up that his size was in the 95th percentile, just as Jacob's had been, I didn't feel victorious, I felt wistful. My little baby was slipping away already, turning into someone bigger.

If Jacob's babyhood gave me an appreciation of the miracle of growing independence, Liam's is teaching me that dependence is equally miraculous. I nurse Liam without wondering when he'll be weaned, and rock him before bed without being concerned that he learn to fall asleep on his own. I look into his eyes, and think with amazement that he doesn't know how to talk, he can't even say one word, and that somehow, despite this glaring deficit, he can communicate all his needs. I put him on a blanket in the middle of our family room and he is happy to lie on his back, smiling at the ceiling fan. With Jacob, I might have whipped out a toy or a book so that he could learn something while he was lying there. With Liam, I find myself more apt to look up at the ceiling fan with him. And seeing the fan through the eyes of someone who has never seen one before, I recognize that it is mysterious and beautiful.

I find myself simply enjoying Liam for who he is: a two-month-old baby who smiles and flails his arms and looks around with limited neck control. In the next month, he will probably figure out that he can reach for the things he wants, but I'm in no hurry for that to happen, for there is a certain peace in holding a baby who is too young to do anything besides relax against my body. Liam is dependent on his father and me in a way he will never be again. And while I am happy when he lifts his head higher than he did the day before and makes eye-contact while cooing, I am just as happy when he sleeps in my arms like he did when he was only hours old.

As I revel in the non-milestones of Liam's life, I am trying to teach myself to do the same for Jacob. I watch him ride his tricycle and strain not to think about the two-wheeler he might have next year. I pull my mind back from imagining his first day of kindergarten. I hold him as he cries, and swallow my words of "you're too big." And as I do these things, I give thanks for this second baby of mine, not a rerun at all, who is teaching me that childhood is not about milestones and accomplishments. It's about being a child.

ॐ   ॐ   ॐ

I give thanks for the unique gift of each of my children. Guide me to understand that each child will teach me something different about being a parent.

CHAPTER TWO

Having Trouble Being a Baby

*F*our-week-old Liam was having a very difficult day. By 10 A.M., he was on his fifth outfit, having spit up more milk than I would have believed my breasts could produce in one morning. He was crying off and on, and I was not sure why. Jacob, three, watched as his brother screamed. Jacob had been asking me what was wrong every five minutes for the last hour, and I had been answering him with guesses as to what the problem might be. Liam was hungry. Liam spit up. Liam needed changing. Liam needed to be burped.

Finally, annoyed with Jacob because of all the questions, and Liam because of all the crying, I blurted,

"Liam is having trouble being a baby."

"Oh," Jacob replied, as if this made perfect sense. He went back to his trucks, and despite the fact that Liam didn't calm down for another half hour, Jacob did not question me again.

At the time, I didn't even know what I meant when I said that Liam was having trouble being a baby. Later I realized that in my frustration, I had stumbled upon a truth.

He was having trouble being a baby.

13

Just a month ago, Liam was not a baby—not really. He was a fetus. His food and oxygen were delivered through an umbilical cord and there was no need to eat or breathe. He lived in a warm, wet, quiet place, where he had been held tightly and rocked for the past nine months. There were no clothes there; no diapers; no changes. There was no need to burp, and nothing to spit up. While relatives joked about what a tough life a newborn had, all eating and sleeping, it was in fact, a tough life compared to his blissful floating in the womb.

And now, one month into his first experience with gravity, air, temperature changes and hunger, my tiny son was having trouble being a baby.

Jacob, by virtue of being three, had understood what I meant even before I did. Things were not so simple for Jacob, either, I realized. Within the last year, just as he had become comfortable with leaving the last vestiges of babyhood behind, new responsibilities emerged—going on the toilet, saying please and thank you, getting dressed. Jacob probably understood Liam's difficulty being a baby because sometimes he had trouble being a three-year-old.

Talking to my husband about it later, we discussed how easy it was to look at a stage long left behind and think of it as problem-free. As a couple, we often caught ourselves reminiscing about how simple our life was before kids. In our blurred memories, it was a carefree time, filled with late nights and romantic dinners. Struggling to deal with the demands of two small children, we conveniently forgot the difficulties of our early marriage; the frustrations that came with trying to blend two lives together, the questions about careers, and the multitude of other issues that time somehow ironed out for us.

If we were able to forget the obstacles that faced us only five years ago, weren't we also likely to look at the lives of our children without recognizing their struggles?

"He's having trouble being a baby," became our operative phrase. We understood it to mean that right now, Liam was trying to learn something about his world and it was difficult for him, just as difficult as it had been for us to land jobs or balance our checkbook just a few years ago.

Hearing us use the phrase, Jacob picked it up, and often would ask it as a question.

"Are you having trouble being a baby today, Liam?" he would ask his brother, stroking his newborn cheek or grasping Liam's hand in his own.

The phrase diffused bouts of crying, helping us to remember that for Liam, being wet or hungry was a problem that seemed to have no solution in sight. "He's having trouble being a baby" gave me the insight to realize that sometimes Liam just needed to be held; not because anything was wrong, but rather because his life experience prior to babyhood was one of constant touch. Somehow, the phrase seemed to carry more compassion than saying Liam was fussy or cranky—negative words that implied that if he wanted to, he could change his condition.

As the weeks went by, Liam turned two months, then three, and I found myself using the phrase less and less frequently. Day by day, he seemed to be finding it easier to be a baby. He started smiling at anyone who made eye contact with him, as if to show just how much he was learning. I rarely had to change his outfit because of a spit-up, and he let me know he needed a feeding or a fresh diaper with small whimpers rather than frantic screams.

I looked into his eyes one morning when he was being especially delightful, and was amazed at the new baby confidence I saw there.

"You're not having much trouble being a baby anymore," I said to him. He stuck his fist in his mouth and cooed back at me. And I wondered if he was proud of me, as well. I wasn't having as much trouble being a mom.

❧　　❧　　❧

Loving God, give me the patience to look at
my children's struggles through their eyes,
rather than my own.

CHAPTER THREE

Extra Large

*S*ometimes I want a little baby. A tiny little baby to cradle in one arm and dress in newborn outfits. I want to marvel at itsy-bitsy fingers and teensy toes. I want strangers to come up to me and ooooh and ahhhh because it is not every day that you see someone so small. It's not that I'm still waiting for my first baby. I have two young boys. The thing is, they were only tiny for a week. Jacob was eight pounds at birth and Liam was nine pounds. With each of them, I reveled in their sheer smallness at the time. I remember holding Jacob's newborn foot up to my husband's size-13 shoe and feeling like it was almost impossible that a person could be so small and still have all the necessary parts for life. When Liam was born, I cupped his head in my hand.

Neither boy was content to stay in the single digits of weight for long, though, and by their first pediatric visits, only a week or so after birth, both were a solid ten pounds. By the time they were two weeks old, newborn-size clothes fit like sausage casings. Some babies have trouble learning to nurse. Not my boys. Both latched on efficiently in the hospital and sucked their way to the top of the size range for babies their age. When I took Jacob in for his six-week checkup, I undressed him and put him on the scale. His chubby arms and legs kicked furiously and his belly quivered.

"What a giant baby," the nurse said as she tapped the scale to fourteen pounds. "What kind of formula is he on?"

"No formula. Just breast milk," I said.

"This is all breast milk?" She sat Jacob up and rolls of baby fat settled above his diaper as she fastened it. "Usually breast-fed babies are a little smaller than average. He's in the 99th percentile for both length and weight."

Jacob kept growing at this clip and was toddler-sized long before he could toddle. Since he didn't take his first steps until he was almost 15 months old, and didn't grow a full head of hair until even later, he had an unusual look.

"It looks like he's pretending to be a baby," a friend said to me as we sipped coffee at a mothers' group one day. The other just-turned-one-year-olds, all smaller than Jacob, were cruising around the room, holding on to furniture or taking a few running steps and falling. Jacob was crawling after them in delight.

"He is a baby," I said.

It was conversations like this that have made me want to slow down the growth of my husky boys. Inside those big bodies are two little kids, and I don't want anyone to forget that. I am afraid that because Jacob, now four, is taller than other kids his age, he will be expected to act older, too. A friend of mine with a five-year-old who is quite a bit shorter than Jacob confessed that she was surprised to see Jacob crying when his block tower fell down. It took her a moment to remember that Jacob was a full year younger than her child, and that tears of frustration aren't too unusual for the pre-kindergarten set.

But it is not just the expectations that others might place on my boys which causes me to be wistful. Some of it is simply about size. A couple down the street have a 17-month-old girl, Tyra, who is smaller than seven-month-old Liam. Little Tyra stretched out her time as an infant; it seemed to me that her parents had a newborn for five or six months, rather than a week or two like we did. Even now, she seems more like a baby than a little girl. A couple times a week, I see the family taking a walk together, Tyra snug in a pack on her father's back. Ten months from now, when Liam is Tyra's age, the baby backpack will be a distant memory. He is already almost too heavy for it now. And while I am, of course, thankful that Jacob and Liam are growing into robust, healthy boys, I cannot erase that tinge of sadness that my husband and I are only getting a glimpse of their tiny selves while Tyra's parents receive a long gaze.

Despite the constant predictions from relatives about pro football in our family's future, I am trying to remember that my boys, big as they are, are the smallest they will ever be. And knowing this, I am taking the smallness where I can find it. I kiss Liam's chubby cheeks and marvel at his nose, still no bigger than my thumbnail. I lift Jacob up and hold him, just to prove I still can.

The other night, after I finished nursing Liam, Jacob climbed on my lap, and for a few minutes, they were both quiet and still against my body. As I closed my eyes and rocked them, Jacob whispered in my ear, "You're not going to stop doing this are you?"

I shook my head and hugged them tighter. Because on my

lap, rocking in the darkness, smelling like talcum powder and baby shampoo, they didn't seem so big at all.

❧   ❧   ❧

Loving God, give me the wisdom to live in the moment —
to see my children not only as older and bigger than
they have ever been, but also as younger and smaller
than they will ever be again.

CHAPTER FOUR

Shopping for My Boy in the Girls' Department

When Jacob was just beginning to toddle, all of his clothes were cute. Tiny trains made their way across the front of his overalls. Smiling lions peeked out from pockets. Some of his hats even had ears. A friend of mine has a girl about the same age, Ellie, and her baby clothes were darling as well. Fuzzy kittens, ladybugs, the whole bit. But when Jacob turned three, something changed. While Ellie's clothes continued to sprout animals with big eyes and goofy grins, Jacob's became more subdued. Ellie had bumblebees, elephants and Elmo. Jacob had flannel shirts and jeans.

Shopping for a gift in the little girls' department, I found it bursting whimsical patterns and bright colors. The boys' department, on the other hand, was determined to stay serious, concentrating instead on forest green and all things sports. I was annoyed.

It wasn't that I wanted my son to wear daisies and frills or to be any less masculine. The child exited the womb knowing how to make car sounds, and could hit solid grounders before he was out of diapers. I was fine with that. It was just that when I described him as a little boy, "little" was the operative word, and I wanted his clothing to reflect this. At age three, he had more in common with the drooling baby a few doors down than he did with the preteen boys in their low-riding jeans who skateboarded on our street. And I knew that there was precious little time this would be true.

After looking at one too many rugby shirts one day while folding laundry, I decided to beat the system. Armed with my charge card, I strode into the local department store and headed for the pink sign that said "Girls." After flipping through a few racks of shirts that were too flowery, too frilly, or too pink, I found what I was looking for: a striped blue and white sweater, size four. There were no flowers, no bows, no ruffles. On the front was sewn an adorable fuzzy brown bear. The ears stuck out, and the bear smiled at me shyly as I looked at it. It was the perfect sweater for a three-year-old boy.

Jacob loved the sweater, and so did his buddies on our block. I was hooked. When I wanted a new outfit for him to wear for his first day of preschool, I did only a cursory check of the boys' department, then went to the girls' section and found a navy sweater vest stitched with primary colored ABCs, crayons and pencils. He wore it with a crisp white t-shirt and khaki pants.

When I told my friends about my exciting discovery, showing them my newest find, a red Winnie-the-Pooh sweatshirt, they seemed confused. They wondered why I cared what he wore. I paused at their questions. Why did I care so much? I'm a woman who doesn't know the current fashion trend until it makes its way to the clearance rack. In my free time, I read *Newsweek*, not *Vogue*. Why was I suddenly so concerned about the wardrobe possibilities for young boys?

Upon reflection, I discovered my concerns went deeper than the clothes themselves. What bothers me is the message implicit in the difference between boys' and girls' clothes. The fact that my husband could safely wear a larger size of just about anything in the boys' department, but I'd look ridiculous in adult versions of the little girl clothes tells me that it's okay for girls to be small and cute, but boys are expected to be little men. While strides have been made in the last generation, it's still true that girls can cry when their feelings are hurt, but boys are expected to hold back their tears. Middle school girls take stuffed animals to slumber parties; boys leave theirs in the darkness of their own bedrooms. Studies show that parents tend to hug and touch their little girls more than their boys. And a baby boy might be referred to as a "tough" little guy, but few would use the same adjective for a baby girl. There is something unsettling about these things. All children have the right to be children; to be small and protected, to be vulnerable and un-tough. They need to be able to cry and be held. They need permission to be kids in a world that seems intent on selling adulthood to children.

The flip side of my problem with little boys' clothes, my friends with girls tell me, is that once their girls outgrow size 7, the stores offer them slinky, midriff-baring outfits that would be more appropriate on a rock stage than a playground. Should these moms visit the boys' department for some solid-colored turtlenecks to wear under those outfits? Yikes.

As far as four-year-old Jacob is concerned, Girls 4-7 continues to offer strong possibilities occasionally. While I know that bright colors and ABCs won't change everything, a fuzzy bear on the front of Jacob's sweater might remind me how young he really is; it might make me bend down and scoop him into my arms. Though I may not even be conscious of it, that bear might earn my son an extra hug. And I'll shop for extra hugs in whatever department sells them.

❧   ❧   ❧

Loving God, when society's expectations for
my children don't match my own,
give me the courage to make my own way.

CHAPTER FIVE

Alleluia Kid

I have always marveled at how the Alleluias simply go away during Lent. On Ash Wednesday, they vanish quietly from their usual place before the Gospel and don't emerge again until Easter. Going to church the first Sunday of Lent, I can't help but scan the order of worship in hopes that one snuck by unnoticed by the music minister. A renegade Alleluia tucked into an otherwise appropriately drab and dreary Lenten song. It has never happened. Where do they go? I imagine them crouched in a dark confessional for the 40 days, stifling their excitement and enthusiasm in deference to the solemnity of the season. They are probably wrapped in dark gray wool blankets so their natural light doesn't shine through and accidentally flood the church with bright yellow and pink (the true color of all Alleluias, in case you hadn't known). More than giving up meat on Friday—not so difficult for this semi-vegetarian—I have always had a difficult time giving up Alleluias for Lent. In fact, I don't know that I have ever made it through the entire song "Jesus Christ has Risen Today" on Easter morning without getting choked up on the Alleluias that follows each line, so happy am I to get them back.

But, this year is going to be different. This year, I have an Alleluia-ing two-year-old little boy at home who is no more likely to give up the word for Lent than he is to start saying, "Yes Mama," when I ask him to clean up his blocks.

I'm not sure exactly when Liam decided to make Alleluia a part of his vocabulary. Overall, he is not a toddler quick to pick up new words. Generally, his motto for talking has been: "Why talk when you can run around and jump off the couch?" Neither my husband nor I use Alleluia around the house — despite my attachment to the word, I have rarely said it or sung it outside of church.

Liam is another story. He sprinkles Alleluias like sugar over the events in his day. He uses the word correctly, and in context. True to church tradition, Liam avoids simply saying the word in a normal voice, but rather yells it, sings it or chants it. He can't say the "L" sound, so his version is actually "A-yay-yoo-ya." The Catholic Church's Vatican II proclaimed the vernacular, or native tongue, holds precedence. Liam always speaks in his native tongue.

My guess as to how he picked up the word has to do with the many Sundays he has spent sitting on my lap in church. From little on, Liam has always been a baby on the move, and keeping him contained and still through the first reading, Psalm response and second reading has been an exercise in upper arm strength and a testament to the staying power of Cheerios. By the time the congregation stands for the Gospel Acclamation, Liam is ready to dance. Or run away. The upbeat Alleluias favored by our church have always been a perfect compromise. Since Liam was about five months old, I've held him facing the altar, swaying to the music. I've pumped his chubby legs in rhythm to the beat, and have blessed his head, mouth and heart with the three crosses when we are finished with the Acclamation. I think he learned that Alleluia must be one exciting word if it can bring so much action to a morning of sitting around.

Liam's Alleluias outside of church spout out spontaneously. Going to Grandma and Grandpa's often warrants Alleluia-singing for several blocks beforehand. Once, after a particularly difficult evening, Liam's restlessness was finally assuaged by the consumption of a large piece of bundt cake. This brought on an Alleluia that had some similarity to a wolf howl. His first poop on the potty was followed by a chorus of Alleluias emitted during a celebratory slide down the stairs.

If the standing Alleluia of the Gospel Acclamation calls us to pay special attention to the words of Jesus, Liam's Alleluias during the day make me focus on God's presence in day-to-day life. Liam's Alleluias remind me that snow is a miracle. That eating noodles should be a joyful occasion. That there is something strange and wonderful about squirrels and bath bubbles and drinking from a straw.

And as Lent begins and the Alleluias in church fade away, my Alleluia-ing boy will still be going strong. Reminding me that while a 40-day desert stay is one way of finding God, another way is to look deeper into the ordinary and pull out joy. Alleluia.

❦   ❦   ❦

Loving God, inspire me to see you in the ordinary;
help me to rediscover my own enthusiasm
through my children's wonder.

CHAPTER SIX

A Third?

*L*iam is napping and Jacob is in school and I'm thinking of another baby again. These "third baby" thoughts rarely come when the boys are fighting or I am awakened in the middle of the night by someone who needs a drink or fell out of bed. The thoughts of baby number three come when the house is quiet; when Jacob puts his arm around his little brother and kisses him; when Liam tells me he loves me "this much" and holds out his little arms just as far as he can. My third baby thoughts come during those times that it seems that my boys are growing so fast I can almost see their pants getting shorter as they stand in front of me. They come when I pick up six-year-old Jacob from school and I look at an eighth grader towering over his mother and realize that, God-willing, my son will stand taller than me in fewer years than I would have believed possible when I held him as a wrinkled newborn.

When my husband Bill and I got married, we had not talked about what size our family would be. My surprise pregnancy with Jacob happened before we could get to the family-size discussion, and once we had Jacob, it never occurred to me that we would have any fewer or more than two babies. Bill and I each have one sister and having two children seemed natural — a given almost. When Liam was a baby, I would look at other moms I knew with three or four, and in one case, five children, and not understand what drove people to have more than two children. To me, two children were children enough.

One child seemed like a lonely idea, but three or more meant that parents played zone defense rather than man-to-man. With baby Liam and preschooler Jacob, I saw no need to make more work for ourselves.

Something changed within me as Liam approached his third birthday and I'm still not sure what it is. We went to the beach with some friends, and I had so much fun with my wet, slippery boys, that I began to think that I didn't want this pudgy, innocent stage to end so soon. I splashed Liam in the water and watched Jacob practicing his very shaky front crawl and wanted the day to last forever. On that hot summer afternoon, it seemed to me that in just a whisper of time passing, my boys would be floating away into the deeper water. And while I didn't want to prevent them from growing up, it occurred to me that I could have another one. That I was allowed to have another one. I had never before stretched my mind around the idea of a third bed, a third car seat — or most exciting, a first pink dress — and letting my imagination go to a future I had never before considered was exhilarating.

Bill understands these baby-longings of mine, and is especially attuned to the fact that a part of the baby longings, might be, more specifically, baby-girl-longings. But when Bill looks at the possibility of another child for us, he sees the thousands of U.S. children languishing in foster care, waiting for a mom or a dad to call their own. He sees one of these children as our first responsibility as a family. To him, implicit in every Gospel is the command to move outside of ourselves—and foster care would widen our circle.

And I have no argument. Our family is healthy and happy and whole. Our children are well-behaved; they seem well-adjusted and secure. We have enough money and enough room. Part of our wedding vows included a promise to always reach out to others, and we both recognize there would be no greater way to reach out than to welcome an abandoned or abused child into our family.

And yet.

That's all I can say. The yets add up in my mind. And yet I would love to see a daughter who has my hair or my laugh. And I'm not sure I want to complicate our lives with the problems that foster care could bring. And I feel like life is getting shorter by the day, and if I think for even a second that I want to have a third child, we should, because someday we won't be able to.

But if I felt a "yes I do," instead of a "I think I might," Bill would jump in with few questions. Each time I see a foster care case in the headlines, I can't help but think, "We could do that," and know there would be less chance we would if we have another biological child. And when Liam dumps his breakfast on the floor or Bill and I go days without an uninterrupted conversation, I'm not sure if I want one more little person around the house—biological or not. I had both children before I was 30, ahead of many of my friends. In doing so I exchanged the freedom of my twenties for the responsibilities of parenthood. I don't have any regrets, but now, with freedom coming back in small tastes—a night out here, a weekend away there, do I want to give up my thirties as well?

My mind and heart are a tangle and I oscillate so wildly that I fear I am making Bill dizzy. The thought of becoming pregnant today fills me with equal parts trepidation and joy. I am so happy with our family as it stands. I have this feeling that we may be complete. But within this sense of completeness hovers the vision of soft baby cheeks, fuzzy footed pajamas and one more chance to shape a life. Maybe a life that comes from my own womb. Maybe a life that has its start outside of me.

With no clear answers in sight, I am cradling both the idea of a third child, as well as the possibilities that will come if we choose not to have another. And as our household sleeps, I often awaken, just as I used to when the boys were tiny. Alone in the darkness, I ask God to nurse these questions of mine; to rock our family's future, whatever it may hold.

❧   ❧   ❧

Loving God, I give you my deepest questions.
Lead me where you want me to go.

CHAPTER SEVEN

Dear Daughter-in-Law

*D*ear Future Daughter-In-Law,

I have a three-year-old boy named Liam and someday he will be your husband. Since Liam's birth, I find my mind skipping far into the future, and in this future, I imagine you. I find myself wondering where you are, if you're born yet, if you're still floating in the womb, if you have yet to be conceived. For all I know, future daughter-in-law, I've driven past a soccer field as you kicked the winning goal or passed you in the mall while you were snoozing in your stroller. While I don't know who you are, or where you are, I do know that if my son chooses to marry, you will be the most important person in his life, and that fills me with awe.

When Liam was a baby, his older brother, Jacob, (your future brother-in-law), asked me where Liam was before he was born. I told him that he was up in heaven with the other babies who were waiting for families.

"We sure were lucky to get him," Jacob said. I looked at little Liam sitting on my lap, and agreed with Jacob. We were lucky indeed.

What was your first meeting like? Was it one chance in a thousand? Isn't it overwhelming to think of how close you were to not meeting at all? I don't believe your meeting Liam was a random thing, any more than I believe his conception was random. I haven't got it all figured out, but I believe there is a plan at work.

By the time I meet you, future daughter-in-law, Liam and I will have had our share of ups and downs. I don't imagine that we will be able to get through little boyhood, adolescence and young adulthood without some arguments and tears. We've had some already. You will know me only through my son's grown-up eyes. And that's why I'm writing to you. I want you to know of this magical time in Liam's life, a time he will have only as a fuzzy memory. And maybe also, I want to show you—the most precious, central woman in my son's life—a time when I was that woman.

Liam has a gentle spirit about him that I pray will not be squashed by the rough and tumble world of boys. He curls up on my lap and quietly chants "cuddle, cuddle, cuddle," as I rock him. At lunch today, I shared my bowl of chicken and rice soup with him and he told me he loved me as he slurped down a carrot. He has soft lips and hair that smells like either raisin bran or grape jelly depending on what time of day it is. He laughs hard, long and often, and he has a little pot-belly that actually does jiggle. But when he doesn't get his way, he does this annoying squawking-screaming thing. My husband and I are trying to teach him to use words when he gets mad, and we make him say he's sorry after a time-out. He can't say the "r" sound, so he says "sowwee."

I hope he's still laughing hard and long when you get married, and that he tells you he loves you not just on candlelight-dinner nights, but also over chicken soup from a can. I hope by the time you marry, Liam hasn't forgotten how to cuddle, and that he has learned to talk out his problems. Most importantly, I hope he can apologize without being reminded, and that every "sorry" is loud, clear and heartfelt.

Future daughter-in-law, I know you aren't wondering about me like I am about you. I didn't think much about my relationship with my own mother-in-law when I got married. I knew, of course, that she was the woman who nursed my husband as an infant and cared for his scrapes and bruises as a child, but because I was not yet a mother, I could not understand what it meant to love someone even before they can love you back.

I took for granted the grace with which my own mother-in-law stepped aside to allow me to be front and center in her son's life. It was a necessary step, and the right step, but amazing nonetheless. My own stepping aside someday will be another way of loving Liam. I hope I can do it as well as my husband's mother.

Future daughter-in-law, you will never know the aspects of Liam I know right now; this part of him that is so full of joy and potential. It will be hard for you to imagine this grown man you love playing with Fisher-Price toys or sleeping on the floor, rather than his bed, because he is pretending to be a lemur in the wild. You will never know what it's like to listen to Liam sing his before-dinner prayer, making it up as he goes along. And I will never fully know the man you know; the grown-up Liam with secrets, prayers and dreams he will share only with his wife.

But as you glimpse little Liam through my words, and I as learn of grown-up Liam through your stories, I know we will both end up with something greater than we had before we met.

Together we hold the two pieces of the Liam we both love. I look forward to seeing the whole picture someday.

See you in twenty or thirty years. You're in my prayers.

Love,

Annemarie, your future mother-in-law

❅   ❅   ❅

Loving God, help me to prepare my children well
for the relationships that they will one day enter into.

PART II:

*Racing through
Early Childhood*

CHAPTER EIGHT

Fears of Abduction

*E*ver since becoming a mother, news about child abductions have jumped out at me from the morning paper. Each case, whether local or not, leaves me nauseated and afraid. For awhile, I reacted to the stories as if my responsibility as a mother was to assume an abduction could happen to my two boys — ages 7 and 4—anywhere, anytime. I hovered on the porch as they played in front of the house. I took note of unfamiliar cars in our neighborhood. Bill and I reviewed the "don't go with strangers" rule and rehashed our "these body parts are private" discussions. We amended our talks about being nice to everyone and gave our usually-polite little boys permission to yell and scream and bite and kick if anyone ever tried to take them. Mostly, we walked the tightrope between not scaring the boys with too much information and giving them enough to offer some protection.

Protection. The more I thought about the role my husband and I have as our children's protectors (in addition to being their cooks, garbage collectors, chauffeurs and entertainers), the less likely abduction by a stranger seemed and the more likely abduction by society in general became. While strangers snatching children is still so rare and terrible that it makes front-page news, the abduction of a child's value system is so common, many of us don't see it anymore.

I decided I needed to be less worried about some nameless villain lurking in the shadows and more worried about the dominant American culture kidnapping the souls of my sons.

Every generation of parents has had its own enemy to fight in terms of protecting their young. Ages ago, cold winters, starvation and wild animals posed the biggest danger to children. In the more recent past, parents were terrified of polio. Today, the biggest threats to our children are insidious and in disguise. Materialism, consumerism, and a culture that glorifies violence, casual sex and self-centeredness prey on our children on a daily basis.

For the first time in human history, many stand to gain more — at least in the short term — by corrupting children than by caring for them.

There is money to be made in selling children toys they don't need and clothes that will go out of style in six months; in convincing them to buy food that corrodes their arteries and entertainment that corrodes their minds. There is money to be made in taking teens' natural interest in sex and using it to sell everything from CDs to TV shows to glossy girls' magazines. Too many stand to make a huge profit if they can convince children that in all things, more is not enough.

I realized, as I watched my little boys play in the front yard, that the Gospel values of living simply, caring little for possessions and reaching out to the marginalized are not only different than the values of society at large, but are actually at odds with those values. And that is where abduction comes in.

Because in order for big corporations to convince my sons that they need to watch a cartoon with rude or violent characters, buy countless plastic action figures or judge people by the brands they are wearing, they will first need to convince my children that the values they have been taught at home are wrong. They will need to steal our family's — our faith's — teachings. And they are working hard to do it — with clever billboards, slick commercials, and even by using those children whose value systems they have already stolen.

But my husband and I, and many parents we know, are working just as hard. Having been given the gift and responsibility of parenthood, we are holding tight to our children, even as our culture strains to pull them from us. We are seeing through the empty promises of commercials and are teaching our children to do the same. We are deciding that driving past is often better than driving "thru." We are acting as guardians and protectors of our children — making decisions about what music, TV programs and clothes are welcome in our home — and which are not. And most importantly, we are making choices in our own lives that teach our children that we value helping people and protecting the earth over buying more and more stuff.

And yet, I know no matter what we do, it is still possible that our children's values may be abducted, for there are no guarantees. We offer them the best protection we know and send them out into the world — and we pray they will not be taken.

❦   ❦   ❦

*Loving God, You have given me the responsibility of
being my children's protector. Help me to keep them safe
from all who seek to exploit them.*

CHAPTER NINE

Oh Yeah, Life Goes On . . .

"*L*ittle ditty about Jack and Diane. Two American kids growin' up in the heartland." John Mellencamp's popular song makes me uneasy. Whenever it comes on the radio as I'm making the bed or driving the kids to school, I stop and listen. And the refrain that comes shortly after that famous beginning always startles me. Makes me swallow hard. Makes me bite my lip and check to see if it is true for me yet.

Oh yeah, life goes on,
Long after the thrill of livin' is gone.

Part of me wants to believe there is no truth to the lyric at all—that life gets more exciting the older you get, with the golden years—not the teenage ones—topping out as the best. But another part of me hears the reality in the lines. There is something unequivocally thrilling about being young. I see it in my own children. Liam actually starts to bounce when he is offered sprinkles on his vanilla ice cream cone, and Jacob yowls in delight at the announcement of a family walk to the park. Children's developmental changes between birth and young adulthood mean that every year they are doing things they have never done before, whether it's riding a two-wheeler or catching a football or kissing someone for the first time.

And even if they have had ice cream with sprinkles or walks to the park before, they have surely not had them hundreds of times. They are in their first round of these little treats. And that's why it's thrilling.

Parents have the privilege of some vicarious thrills. Listening to Jacob read his first book, beginning to end, would fall into the "thrilling" category for me. And anyone with a toddler knows the oddly triumphant feeling that comes from witnessing the first tinkle in the potty.

While experiencing second-hand thrills through my children is undoubtedly one of the sweetest parts of parenting, Mellencamp's song reminds me I need to be careful not to allow these second-hand thrills to become my only thrills. My husband and I need to have thrills that are ours alone. And in the midst of a house littered with the socks, toys and grubby fingerprints of small boys, it can seem like personal thrills come few and far between.

Oh yeah, life goes on,
Long after the thrill of livin' is gone.

One reason that childhood and adolescence are arguably more thrilling than adulthood is that children are not allowed to stay in one place for long. First grade is replaced by second and J.V. becomes varsity. Change is a regular part of the life of a child or teen, and change automatically brings challenge. And thrills.

Adults don't have the luxury of someone else moving us along. Whether or not we stay in a job that is comfortable, but too easy, is our own decision. The ruts we often fall into — cooking the same spaghetti recipe every Monday, sticking with the same hobbies or exercise plan, even praying the same way we have always prayed — are ours to keep if we choose. While no one would allow a child to remain in kindergarten a few years because she doesn't want to replace finger painting with reading and math, few question an adult's choice of comfort over challenge.

When Liam was one, Bill left a comfortable position writing ads for the newspaper to go back to school to become a teacher. It wasn't that he didn't like his job; he just had this gnawing feeling that he could be doing more; could be making a bigger difference. We had two financially tight years as he worked part time and went to school, but there was something oddly thrilling about it. There was considerable risk to Bill's decision to become a teacher. We were choosing to lose two years of full-time salary with his decision to go back to school; we didn't know if he would like teaching; and once a teacher, we knew he would make substantially less money than he made at his other job. Yet it was acknowledging these risks and going forward anyway that gave an exciting edge to a time in our marriage that could have been very routine.

We have a magic marker sign, made by Jacob, taped to our pantry door. It says, "Holy Spirit, help us to be brave, strong friends of Jesus." It is decorated with three crosses, a couple stars and yellow zigzags.

That sign has become a prayer to me as well as a challenge. It is also the closest thing I have to a rebuttal to Mellencamp's refrain. By definition, you can't be either strong or brave if you are not doing something difficult. And conquering the difficult is always thrilling.

Jacob's carefully drawn words of "Help us to be brave, strong friends of Jesus" remind me that living as a Christian should be thrilling, because Jesus' way is very different from what is easy and ordinary. The sign tells me that during those times when I wonder if the thrills are fading, I need to delve deeper into what bravery and strength mean in terms of Christianity. For Bill and me right now, this has meant taking classes to become certified to be foster parents.

The problems of foster care scare me. The idea of bringing a child who has only known a life of neglect or abuse into our home is terrifying. And yet underneath my fear, I detect — thrill. The fear is there because I am afraid we will somehow fail this child, that this child could somehow tax our family beyond our capabilities. The thrill is there because we are taking the classes anyway. We are trying something that no one else I know is trying.

I know a couple who, in their early thirties, left stable jobs and took their two young children to Tanzania, Africa, for a couple years of volunteer work. Another couple I know — with five children — regularly opens their home to poor women and their children who need a hot meal or a temporary place to stay. No worry about the "thrill of livin' " leaving anytime soon for these two families.

Every thrill starts with fear. The thrilling moment comes when we break through that fear — the moment we decide: "I'm frightened, but I'm going forward anyway."

And when this decision to go forward despite fear is applied to following the teachings of Jesus — to loving others, to standing up for justice, to serving the poor — we become both brave and strong. We become people alive with the thrill of Gospel living.

⚮   ⚮   ⚮

Loving God, keep me from falling victim
to my own routine. Give me the courage to
go forward when I am fearful.

CHAPTER TEN

Ash Wednesday

*J*acob received ashes this past Ash Wednesday for the first time. And I wept.

I didn't expect for it to be such an emotional experience. After all, receiving ashes is not a sacrament, and children much younger than first-grade Jacob often receive them as they stand next to their parents. But as a preschooler and kindergartner, little Jacob had hid his face behind my leg as I received my ashes, so that the unfamiliar minister could not mark his forehead. This Ash Wednesday, though, Jacob was not with me for Mass. He was with his class, and I was a dozen pews behind him, with the rest of the parents. There would be no leg to hide behind.

As Jacob approached the sixth grade teacher to receive his ashes, I was one aisle over, in line for my own ashes, watching him.

Remember you are dust, and to dust you shall return.

Dust. In moments, the teacher was going to tell my son he was dust, and that he would return to dust someday. The teacher was going to tell Jacob he would someday die. And standing in line to receive my own ashes, I knew she was speaking the truth. But hearing the words repeated over and over as each person before me received his or her ashes, I recognized that I held in my heart the tiniest hope that this phrase would not be true for my son. That Jacob would somehow beat the system. That he would not suffer and die like the rest of us. That maybe, if Bill and I could just love him enough, dust-to-dust would not apply.

Remember you are dust, and to dust you shall return.

In his homily, the priest had explained the phrase to the children by saying we are only on Earth a certain amount of time. He had held his hands about three feet apart, emphasizing with each hand the beginning and the end of life. During this life, he said, Jesus wants us to be the very best disciples we can be. The ashes remind us we only have a short time to do this.

And as I looked at Jacob, now just three children away from receiving his ashes, I suddenly realized that his time to be a disciple had already begun. He was old enough to understand Father's homily; old enough to understand about life being about 80 years if you're lucky and possibly much shorter. He was old enough to start being a disciple.

And that's when my tears welled. For there is something wonderful and terrible about watching someone you love become a disciple. Being a follower of Jesus is never easy, if you do it right. And to invite a child to become a disciple is to invite that child to enter into some of the suffering that discipleship requires. Parental love made me want to shield my son from any pain. Christian love called me to help him learn to live his life in a rhythm of continual dying and rising with Christ.

Earlier, on the way to school, Jacob and I had talked about the rice that he and his classmates would have for lunch that day as part of Operation Rice Bowl. The money saved from not buying the regular school menu items would be given to the poor. As I drove, we talked about the circumstances of the children in the world who do not get enough to eat each day. I asked Jacob why he thought we chose to eat just rice, and didn't simply eat our regular food, and give the same amount of money to the poor. How can your hunger help kids so far away? I asked. Troubled, Jacob thought for a moment, then said that maybe if we were hungry after lunch because of just eating rice, we would understand a little how it must feel to be hungry all the time, and maybe we would help more because of it.

Old enough to understand. Old enough to be a disciple.

And so, my son stepped forward to receive his ashes. And I stood, watching—somehow as both parent and fellow journeyer. Dust to dust, dear Jacob. Life is so short. Live as a disciple.

✄   ✄   ✄

*Loving God, You have entrusted me with these children.
In turn, I offer them to the world as disciples.*

CHAPTER ELEVEN

Cut-up Hot Dogs: Holy Work

When I am looking for inspiration on becoming a better parent, my parish priest is not the first resource I usually think of. While we have two excellent priests at our parish, the fact remains they are celibate males, and therefore rarely have to say things like "Don't lick the window," or "Remember, you need to lift up the toilet seat before you start going."

Some may argue that a priest who has never had to utter either of these statements can indeed preach effectively to those of us who must say them on a regular basis, but I have never been so sure. Following Jesus when you are only responsible for yourself is difficult enough. Following Jesus when your nerves are frayed because your baby will only sleep if you are standing up and swaying at 3:00 A.M. is another thing entirely.

So when I went to Mass two Sundays ago, I did not expect the homily would be the clearest explanation tying together parenthood and being a follower of Christ that I had ever heard.

I don't remember how Father Joe began his homily. By the time the Gospel ended, I was in the back of the church pacing back and forth with our new foster daughter, Lucinda, age 15 months. We had gone through all toys and books of interest during the opening prayer, a Ziplock bag of Mini-Wheats during the first two readings, and a half bottle of milk during the Gospel. As Father Joe started the homily, Lucinda was frantically kicking her arms and legs in need of some motion.

So I took my place in the very back of the church, pacing, as Father Joe spoke. Lucinda, comforted by the step-step-bounce pattern of my walk, relaxed in my arms and I could listen.

In the Gospel, Jesus had cured a leper, and in doing so, became so sought after that he could barely walk through the town. In taking away some of the leper's pain, Jesus, in essence, brought discomfort and pain upon himself. This is what being a Christian means, Father Joe said. In an effort to lessen another's pain, we take some of their pain on ourselves. He said that parents do this constantly—a parent will stay up with a sick child—and in the process often become sick, too—so that the child is not alone in his or her sickness. A parent will listen to a child's sorrow, and take some of that sorrow as his or her own so as to lighten the child's burden. In doing this, he said, parents are acting as true followers of Christ.

As I walked with Lucinda, Father Joe gave other examples, but I hung onto the ones about parenting. Lucinda had come into our lives about ten days earlier, part of the Milwaukee County child welfare system. Her arrival, while very welcome, had rocked our world. Full nights of sleep were now a hazy memory, and our small Toyota Corolla seemed to have shrunk two sizes with the addition of another car seat. The constant motion of a toddler added intensity to our already-busy family life. But implicit in Father Joe's words, was that our family took a hit of instability so that Lucinda's life could be more stable.

I thought of my friend Patty, mother of five, who had told me about an argument she helped work out with her ten-year-old twins. She had known the twins were angry with one another, and she acted as a facilitator to their argument, allowing each twin to say what she needed to say, but preventing the fight from getting ugly or out of hand. Patty absorbed and diffused some of their anger. In choosing to become involved in their conflict, Father Joe would say she acted as Jesus, releasing some of her daughters' tension by taking it on herself.

The reason parenting is so exhausting is that we are living our own lives plus those parts of our children's lives that they are not up to yet. Every fanny wiped, every hot dog cut into small bits, every comforting hug after a nightmare is a way of taking a child's difficulty and making it our difficulty. Parenting is the constant shelving of our own wants in favor of a child's needs. And the twist that makes it even more difficult is what we know is best for our children is not always what they themselves want. Parenting would be almost easy if children's wishes reigned—four or five hours of TV a day, lots of junk food, no bedtime, no vegetables, no need to get dressed or be anywhere on time. The "no's" we say, the limits we set, and the anger or tears or pouts we encounter because of those no's and limits are also part of being Christ to our children. We absorb the momentary fury of a child rather than compromise that child's future growth, health or development.

When Mass ended, I tried to thank Father Joe for his homily, but could just manage a few words before I had to run after Lucinda, who, exhilarated with the freedom of finally being put down, was careening toward the steps. I caught her before she fell, helped Liam blow his nose, and held Jacob's books while he zipped his jacket. I glanced at a nearby mother who was bundling her baby before going out into the cold. She nodded at me and smiled. Our work was holy.

❧ ❧ ❧

Loving God, help me to see parenting as a ministry —
a way of being Christ to my children.

CHAPTER TWELVE

Delivering Lucinda

We never left the honeymoon stage with our first foster daughter, Lucinda. She wasn't with us long enough. Lucinda arrived the day after Jacob's eighth birthday. He told me later that when he blew out his candles, he had wished that a foster child would come very soon. At the time of his birthday, we had been certified foster parents for a week and had missed several calls to take children. Social workers would call us for a placement when we weren't home, leave a message, but then move on down the list of available foster parents who could handle emergency placements. Coming home to the broken dial tone of the voicemail was nerve-wracking.

"Hello, this is Kara, from Child Protective Services. We have Kevin, a two-year-old boy who needs placement tonight. Could you give us a call back?"

"We have a two-month-old on a heart monitor and we're wondering if you'd be open to that?"

"I know you're only certified for one child, but we're looking for a placement for twins."

They had always found someone by the time I called back.

But the day after Jacob's birthday, we were home when the phone rang. Four children were being removed from a home because of neglect. They would drop the youngest off in an hour. Bill called his sister to ask if she would pick up some diapers for us, and I ran around the house, frantically cleaning. Jacob whipped out his homework and got to work, so he wouldn't miss any of the action when the baby came.

The doorbell rang as I shoved the last pair of boots into the closet, and the boys rushed to open the door. A social worker stood there, holding a crying one-year-old. Lucinda. Another social worker waved to us from the front seat of a minivan in our driveway where she sat with the other children.

The first social worker handed the baby to me. Lucinda was chubby and small for her age. Her two front teeth were chipped and I couldn't tell if the red mark on the side of her face was a rash or a large birthmark. I stroked her fine, wavy black hair as we sat down at the dining room table to fill out paperwork. Both my boys had still been bald at fourteen months and Lucinda's hair was already almost shoulder length. Long enough to put in a bow. As I held her, Lucinda's cries turned to soft whimpers, then subsided completely, and I couldn't help but note this was my easiest delivery. No contractions.

After we completed the paperwork, the social worker handed us a small, ripped plastic bag.

"This was all we could find for her," she said. I pulled out a kids size-four sweatshirt. I looked at Lucinda. She probably wore an infant size 12 months, at the most.

Bill and I went outside so Lucinda could say goodbye to her siblings. Her sisters and brother were crying in the backseat and I promised them we would take good care of Lucinda.

Just four, six and nine, how could they understand what was happening?

"I will rock her in a rocking chair, and I'll give her good food, and I'll change her diaper," I told them. "We have a lot of toys that she can play with. We will make sure she's happy." I didn't know what else to say.

I wiped my eyes and Bill gave them a box of fruit snacks, a bag of cookies and some juice boxes.

"Shouldn't we be taking them all?" he said to me, turning, so they couldn't hear.

I imagined my own boys in the same situation, in a van with two strangers, being split up and sent to live with other strangers. Wouldn't I want someone to take them both? But it was in thinking of my own boys that I told Bill no.

"I couldn't do it well," I said.

Lucinda stayed with us two weeks and five days. We had been out of the toddler stage for a couple of years, now that Liam was four, and there was something sweet about the return to baby wipes and bottles. Friends responded to Lucinda's arrival with cards and gifts. A couple of them made me meals, even as I protested. Lucinda seemed to adapt to our family life with remarkable ease, except perhaps for fusing to me a bit too tightly, and not letting Bill hold her or even get too close. She would wave to him across the room, however. He waved back. And though she became almost an appendage on my hip, and would only sleep if she were touching some part of me, she was not with us long enough for this to get tiresome. In the not-quite-three weeks we had her, my main concern was to somehow, with constant touch, make up for the lack of touch in her life so far.

The call to retrieve Lucinda came suddenly.

"Lucinda's grandmother is taking all the kids," the social worker said. "Will you be home tomorrow at 3:00 so I can pick her up?"

The day Lucinda was to leave, I came home from dropping Liam off at school and found a gift bag inside the front door. Six darling spring outfits from a friend who hadn't known Lucinda was leaving today. I packed them with her other things.

The social worker came, a twenty-something woman with a cropped shirt, jeans and a pierced belly button. Her outfit bothered me. This baby was once again leaving a family she knew to go live with someone else. Whether or not Lucinda understood it, this was an important day in her life, and somehow, I felt the social worker's clothes did not respect this. Probably, I was angry, but did not know who to be angry at, so I was choosing the pierced navel.

I put Lucinda in the social worker's carseat with a graham cracker and a pacifier. I helped the social worker load all the clothes and toys Lucinda had received as gifts into the trunk. I had remembered to pack the sweatshirt, too. And then I said goodbye. I said goodbye to the daughter who wasn't quite a daughter. To the daughter who was another mother's daughter. I said goodbye to my easiest delivery so far, praying for her grandmother who she would be delivered to next.

I love you, Lucinda.

℘   ℘   ℘

I pray for families —families together and families apart.
I pray for the children who cannot live with their families.

CHAPTER THIRTEEN

How Long? Does It Matter?

*O*ne of the first questions people ask when they meet Tonisha, our 17-month-old foster daughter is, "How long will she be with you?"

It's a natural question, and a good question, but it is one I cannot answer. In our almost three months of being foster parents, one of the things my husband Bill and I have come to learn about the neglected or abused children who are part Milwaukee county's foster care system is that the unknown is a fact of life. How long Tonisha stays in our home is dependent on her birth parents getting their lives back on track to the degree that they are able to care for their children. The attorneys and social workers in charge of Tonisha's case can guess how long this might take, but they don't like to, and the range of their guesses is so wide—"anywhere from three weeks to a year"—that they are better off not making any prediction at all.

So Tonisha is a part of our family for maybe the rest of this month, or maybe the rest of this year, or maybe even—and this would be unlikely—forever, if both her mother's and father's parental rights were to be terminated.

We have a baby living with us and we don't know how long she will stay. Everything is a reminder of the uncertainty of Tonisha's situation. I look at the one-size-too-big shoes we received from a neighbor and wonder if Tonisha will still be with us when she fits into those shoes. I imagine her in a little summer dress, in a swimsuit, or on a family camping trip, without even knowing if she will still be with us when the winter jackets are finally put away.

The uncertainty of Tonisha's situation makes me realize how deeply we depend on what we perceive to be the duration of a relationship to know how to love someone or how much effort to give the relationship. When I talk with other women my age, we agree that it has become more difficult to make close friends as we tick toward the mid-thirty mark. We are so busy, and establishing a new friendship can be an exercise in risking precious time and emotional energy without a definite payoff. So we hold back unless we think the friendship has a chance of progressing and moving forward.

The nature of foster parenting, however, is loving without regard to the future. And it's a different kind of love than I have ever experienced before. From Tonisha's perspective, it doesn't matter whether she stays a month or a year. She just needs her toes kissed and her cheeks stroked. She needs someone to cheer for her as she learns to walk and understand that she means banana when she shouts "'Nana!" If she is clothed, diapered, fed and hugged regularly, she knows she is loved.

Tonisha, at 17 months, cannot understand the uncertainty of her future, and because of this, cannot be concerned about it. And by living so deeply in the present, she helps Bill and me do the same.

Tonisha has made me question the categories I put people into—stranger, acquaintance, close friend, family. If two months ago I didn't even know Tonisha and now she is like a daughter to me, what potential might my other relationships hold, if only I gave them a chance? How many opportunities do I miss for loving others because I am looking towards the future instead of living in the present?

Tonisha reminds me that Jesus' command, "Love one another" does not carry with it the promise of a long-term relationship with the one being loved. "Love one another" is a command made with Jesus' knowledge that when we love people, they flourish. When we love others, they have the opportunity to become, more fully, the people they were created to be. Love, in its purest state, always transforms. But it never guarantees we will have a tomorrow.

Tonisha came to us at age 15 months without shoes and barely able to stand. She had a double ear infection, a scalp infection and sores in her mouth. She had never slept in a crib before and woke every hour of each night. She did not smile for the first two days she was with our family.

Now, she walks well and delights us with her giggly, outgoing personality. Her infections and sores have cleared and she sleeps in her crib all night long. She is happy and content. And while I may never be able to answer the daily question of, "How long will she be with you?" I am able to say that Tonisha has been loved every minute of the nine weeks she has been part of our family. And whether she leaves when she is 18 months old, or stays until she is 18 years, I know she will go out of our home stronger than she was when she came.

As I was writing this, I had to put it aside to work on something else. I hit the "close" button of my document, titled simply "Tonisha," and because I forgot to save, a message flashed on my screen.

"Do you want to save the changes you have made to 'Tonisha'?" it asked.

I pressed yes.

Because I do want to save the changes.

❧   ❧   ❧

Loving God, transform me with your love;
that I might in turn transform others.

CHAPTER FOURTEEN

First Car

I sold my 1988 Chevy Nova today for $358 and a batch of chocolate-covered peanut butter balls. The 1988 Nova was my first car, and I never dreamed when I bought it (used) at age 22 that it would be with me the next twelve years. I could have never guessed that by the time I sold the car, I would be married, with a house, two school-aged boys, a baby foster daughter and a completely different career. If I had any inkling the Nova would last so long and so well, I might not have bought it at all—maybe opting instead for something that had a cup-holder and was any other color besides worm-brown.

The Nova was a simple car when I bought it. Even in 1988, most cars had power steering and air conditioning, two features the Nova lacked. I bought it because it was the cheapest car to get red circles (excellent) for everything, except the exhaust system, in *Consumer Reports*. I figured the lack of power steering, air conditioning, automatic transmission and tape deck would make it lighter, and therefore more fuel-efficient on the highway.

The Nova's simplicity was its best—and some would argue, only—feature. Its brown interior meant I could safely spill coffee a few mornings a week without worrying about stains. (No cup-holder, remember.) Its brown, non-glossy paint job was basically the color of dirt, so while the car never really looked sparkling clean, it didn't need washing very much either. The blandness of the Nova meant I did not worry if I parked it in high crime areas. While friends bought car alarms to protect their investments, I counted on the fact that the Nova was too boring to steal.

The first time I drove my then-boyfriend (now-husband) Bill in the Nova, I got a bit flustered while backing out of the apartment's long driveway and bumped into the side of the building, scratching the car and knocking off the side mirror. Without thinking much about it, I opened the door, grabbed the mirror and continued backing without comment. I knew I would be able to reattach the mirror later with duct tape and wasn't too worried about the appearance of the car. Bill told me later he had never seen someone react so calmly when a part of her car broke off. But it is easy to be calm when you don't really care.

As years went on, Bill and I got married and had one child, then another. I kept thinking we might sell the Nova. But it was so reliable, so handy with its hatchback, and such a gas-sipper, that we could never justify selling it.

I began to really like the Nova for the very things that annoyed me before—the non-power steering made me laugh as I parallel parked, and the toothpick Bill had stuck in the radio to keep it working seemed endearing. The Nova was simple living embodied. And there was something freeing about feeling like we were "getting away" with owning such a small, cheap car while the rest of the world bought their SUVs. Who needs four-wheel-drive when you have front-wheel drive?

But I cannot claim the Nova as my own, anymore. The addition of our foster child and her accompanying car seat was the final straw for the Nova. We needed something bigger. My friend Eric has the privilege of Nova-ownership now. Eric is a bike commuter who wanted a car to use in case of emergency. A friend of mine from college, Eric has known the Nova its whole life, and is the person who taught me how to use its five-speed transmission.

Bill and I bought a minivan. It is not brand new, but it's close enough. It has cup-holders, power steering and these little buttons you keep on your key chain that allow you to unlock the door without touching the car. It's a pretty shade of deep purple, and if I scraped it against a building and knocked off the mirror, I would be very disappointed. I'm afraid I like it too much.

The sale of the Nova marks the end of an era. It was a car that saw me through some of the biggest milestones I will have in my life. And as odd as it may sound, I hope the spirit of the Nova continues to live on in our family. I hope we can continue to look at our possessions as sturdy, reliable things that get a particular job done, but don't hold much weight beyond that. I hope we remember that being dependable is a gift—that how you look isn't as important as whether you are there for people when they have someplace to be on a cold winter morning. I hope we remember that our imperfections aren't tragedies, they are a chance to laugh at ourselves.

As I sit here, eating a chocolate covered peanut butter ball, I know we sold the Nova to Eric for a fair price. But I have an unnerving urge to whisper to my old car. To thank it for its brownness, its steady service, its lack of concern with fashion. I have a strange desire to assure my car I think it is worth much more than $358. But knowing the Nova, it isn't offended by the selling price at all. It has always had its priorities in order. And it is probably glad I got the peanut butter balls.

⚜   ⚜   ⚜

Loving God, help me to value simplicity.

CHAPTER FIFTEEN

Dirt, Noise, and the Y Chromosome

I had not planned to have boys.

When I was a little girl, I spent a fair amount of time playing with dolls, and acquired a new one each birthday and Christmas from ages four to about ten. Two dolls a year for six years is 12 dolls. They were all girls. Most had blond hair, blue eyes, wore pink and were very subdued. (Except Baby Thataway, who, powered by two D batteries in her bottom, could crawl indefinitely until she ran into a wall or refrigerator).

I have one sister, Maureen, and no brothers. After school in the winter, Maureen and I would speak with distaste of boys who would take off their boots and run around the classroom in their tube socks. The boys' socks were always too big, and a couple inches of sock would hang off the end of the their feet, soaking up the dirty melting snow from the classroom floor as they slid around. Some people cannot stand fingernails on a chalkboard. For my sister and me, it was gray, soggy, flapping tube socks.

When I babysat, I preferred the families that had all girls or mostly girls. I found little boys to be messy, loud and generally more trouble than the two dollars an hour I was being paid to take care of them.

So when I imagined myself someday as a mother, the children in my mind's eye were always girls.

And now I have two boys.

At five and eight, my boys are in their prime in terms of little boyishness. Today, during church, Liam matter-of-factly pulled a piece of rope, a glow-in-the-dark frog and a dead cicada from his front pocket. When my boys run on grass, dirt or any soft surface, they feel compelled to slide, fall, tackle or dive. Keeping as much of their bodies in contact with as much of the earth as possible while simultaneously moving forward seems to be the goal. This leads to showers and baths involving heavy scrubbing of all bendable parts on each boy. Whenever they engage in pretend play, it is never about going to the store or taking care of the house. Someone is always in crisis and needs to be immediately and loudly rescued by someone else who has special equipment, special powers or a combination of the two.

And I love it.

There is something about living with two little boys that is akin to living with lion cubs. You are never exactly sure what is going to happen next, and your furniture might get chewed along the way, but you never doubt that you are living where the action is.

My friends who have girls about the same age as my boys say that already, they have dealt with cliques and long, involved stories of recess-time drama.

Jacob's idea of a heart-to-heart talk, on the other hand, is to curl up in bed with me on a Saturday morning and give me a play-by-play of yesterday's lunchtime football game. As someone who remembers her own share of recess-time drama and cliques, Jacob and Liam's world of constant movement and fewer words is refreshing.

My sons' unceasing drive to run, jump, throw and catch has awakened the latent athlete within me. If I want to spend time with my boys, it is not going to be quietly stringing beads together for a craft project. I have developed a pretty good spiral by playing pass with Jacob, and Liam's daring relationship with water has forced me off my towel and into lakes and pools before I even get to my magazine's table of contents.

And now, eight solid years into my adventure with my little XY chromosomes, I have a girl. Tonisha, our foster daughter, will be two next month. She has been with us since she was 15 months old, and while she has obviously been a girl that whole time, babies seem rather androgynous to me. Tonisha's upcoming birthday makes me wonder about the girl aspect of her. Other than the obvious dresses and bows, so far, toddler Tonisha does not seem so different from toddler Liam.

But, if Bill and I should have the privilege of seeing Tonisha grow into a little girl, I wonder what differences we will see between her and our boys?

Strange as it sounds, I believe raising two boys will make me a better mother of a little girl. I already knew about doll buggies, four-square and friendship bracelets. But Jacob and Liam have brought me to the boys' side of the playground. It is rougher and sweatier, but just as fun. And I want to make sure I introduce any daughter of mine to this muddy, wild side of childhood.

A girl in our household—either Tonisha or another foster daughter—will have the advantage of a mom who has been a girl, but has spent the last decade with boys. And while I might play dolls with my daughter, because that is what I know from childhood, I will also teach her to punt a football, because that is what I know from parenthood.

I have to believe that the cliques and recess-time dramas that are part of being a girl will be easier to deal with if you can come home, run around with your brothers, and punt a football. And maybe, the mother-daughter relationship, so tumultuous during the pre-teen and teen years, would be a little easier after a game of one-on-one.

But there is only so far I will go. I'll keep the tube socks out of it.

❧   ❧   ❧

Loving God, your plans for me are so often different
from what I have planned for myself.
I give thanks for what this has brought to my life.

CHAPTER SIXTEEN

Permanent Teeth

I was crossing the playground during recess on my way to the school office last Wednesday when Jacob's permanent teeth ran by.

Jacob was, of course, attached to his permanent teeth, and I am pretty sure my little boy's other body parts ran by as well. But all I saw were his two front permanent teeth. In a strange split second of a mental hiccup, my brain grabbed images of my son at every stage of his life, and I saw baby-toddler-pre-school-second-grade Jacob all at once. But running toward me was the model of Jacob I had originally been given, except now a couple feet taller and with two large teeth where his tiny baby ones had been.

The infant I used to carry tucked snugly in the crook of my arm is now a kid who runs around at recess with permanent teeth. The thought is startling.

I am beginning to realize this growing thing isn't temporary. It keeps happening. Just when I get used to a new phase of parenting, it ends and turns into something else.

For me, parenting started very slowly. I was aware of each day of both my pregnancies' first trimesters; every morning, the clock would creep toward 11 A.M., when the nausea would finally pass. Once the babies were born, an hour pacing or rocking in the middle of the night seemed to contain 90, rather than 60 minutes.

But things started picking up speed after the one-year mark for each of the boys. Rather than anticipating milestones, as I did when I waited for baby Jacob to roll over or for baby Liam to grow hair, the milestones started crashing into me.

Baby books told me what to expect that first year. Peeking ahead, I knew I was supposed to take note of my sons' first smiles, babbles and steps. I waited for these events and duly recorded them on the appropriate pages. Sometimes I wasn't even sure why I was writing them down. How much difference is there, really, between a baby who rolls over and one still working on that skill?

Permanent teeth are endlessly more significant than rolling over, and no one warned me about them. Permanent teeth mark the beginning of the end of cute. While kindergartners, still awaiting their first visit from the tooth fairy, are darling, and first graders, with gaping toothless grins, are simply ravishing, second graders are growing out of cute and into good-looking. You cannot easily scoop a second-grader into your arms.

My son's permanent teeth are his first outward sign of a still-faraway adulthood. While his arms and legs will continue to grow and his face will change as he gets older, his two front teeth are as big as they will ever be. And it makes me wonder what else about him is "permanent." His quiet, thoughtful personality seems pretty well set. He is not one to grab center stage, and I doubt he ever will be. He has loved learning about undersea life for about three years now; I used to think dolphins and whales were a passing phase, but I am not so sure anymore.

I am realizing the milestones of childhood that stand out to me are those moments when I glimpse—if only for a moment—the people my children are becoming. They are the moments I sense "permanency"—when I know that I am not seeing a developmental period that my sons will grow out of, but rather a personality or passion that they are in the process of growing into. Milestones now have less to do with mastery of skills and more to do with emerging values I see—those times when my sons make a choice in behavior that comes not from a fear of a time-out, but rather from a desire to do right. And these moments are not listed in the baby books. They are left for parents to discover at odd times—in unlikely places.

When I left Jacob's school that day, recess was ending, and my son was lined up with his class. The magical baby-toddler-kid was gone, and I once again saw Jacob as I usually do—an eight-year-old with a sprinkling of freckles and smiling hazel eyes. But as Jacob walked into the school, I could not help but think about those permanent teeth. And wonder about the other permanent things I could not see.

૪   ૪   ૪

Loving God, thank you for allowing me to be
the first witness to my child's emerging self.

CHAPTER SEVENTEEN

Priests? My Boys?

*L*ast week I was at the funeral for the father of a dear family friend. Because my friend is a priest, about 25 priests were in attendance at the Mass. After the reception, eight-year-old Jacob, five-year-old Liam and I approached our friend to say goodbye and offer our final condolences. Another priest happened to be standing nearby, and he greeted my sons warmly, asking them where they went to school (they were in their tell-tale Catholic school uniform of navy pants and red shirts.) As this priest shook my sons' hands, he smiled and said, "We have two future priests here, don't we?" He chuckled, looked at me and added that he and my friend were getting older, wouldn't be around forever, and would someday need replacements.

And my hands, which up to that point had been resting lightly on the shoulders of each of my sons, tightened on their own accord. While I smiled back and nodded slightly, "no," was the only word in my mind.

No. You cannot have my sons.

I am not proud of my reaction. But it was honest and true, and I suspect that I am not alone. Another priest friend of mine once explained the current priest shortage this way: "Mothers are not giving their sons to the Church anymore." He said in years past, when Catholic families had six or eight children, parents were more likely to encourage one of the boys to enter the priesthood. Now, with fewer children in a family, parents (and mothers in particular) are reluctant to "lose" a son to the priesthood.

As I drove home, I thought over my reaction to the priest's gentle suggestion that my own boys could become priests someday. It bothered me that my immediate response was a negative one. I am a lifelong Catholic and consider myself very active in the church. Why would I not want my sons to be priests? I had priests to thank for much of my own spiritual development. The poetry, music and homilies of Father Bob Purcell at Marquette University sent me looking for God in all things as a young adult. Father Jack Kern's commitment to care for the poor and oppressed and his Jesus-like countenance were a source of weekly inspiration to my husband and me when we were newlyweds at Saints Peter and Paul Parish. And a succession of Father Bryan Massingale's powerful "live the Gospel, don't just talk about it" homilies actually spurred us on to become foster parents. Why would I not want my sons to become priests like these men?

Part of it is simply because there are so few young men choosing the priesthood these days. The men who do are left without peers in their vocation; all their brother priests are a generation or two older. In the past, the potential loneliness of being a priest was mitigated by larger numbers that gave priests a sense of community or brotherhood. Now, candidates for the priesthood are being asked not only to forsake the opportunity for a wife and children, but to go without a community of peers as well.

What also distresses me as I consider the question of either Jacob or Liam becoming a priest is the fact that my church is eager to receive my sons, but shows little interest in Tonisha. I have four women friends who would make incredible priests—spiritual, caring people, adept at counseling, knowledgeable in theology and excellent public speakers. It troubles me that the Church will look past these women, as well as equally well-qualified married men, in order to maintain the tradition of celibate males leading the flock.

And the recent scandals only add to my hesitation. While great strides have been made in the past two years in righting the wrongs of the past, the Church is still in its infancy in learning to take responsibility for its institutional sins.

And yet, amid all these problems, there is so much I love about the Catholic Church that I understand why young men respond to the call of the priesthood. Each time I receive Eucharist, join hands at the Our Father or am moved into action by a homily, I realize I am one of the many beneficiaries of one person's decision to respond positively to the challenging call of the priesthood.

And even as some of the Church's mistakes get in the way of what I would like the Church to be, I recognize that it is a human organization, made up of human beings who are striving—however imperfectly—to follow Jesus. I recognize that it has been the Church's priests and bishops, along with lay leaders, who have historically brought about change in the Church, and who will continue to do so in the future. Eight years into parenting, I have learned enough to know that God's plan for my sons may be very different than my own. My most important task as a mother is not to tell my sons what to do, but to teach them how to listen for the whisper of the Spirit, so that they might know where they are being led.

Liam told me the other day that when he grows up, he wants to be a builder because, in his words, "I want to love people and take care of them and make sure they have a place to live."

And in the end, if Liam takes this philosophy into his career or vocation, that will be enough for me. The Catholic Church needs good builders—and re-builders—too.

❦   ❦   ❦

Loving God, be with my children as
they discover who they are called to be.

CHAPTER EIGHTEEN

Ten-year Anniversary

On the 21st of each month, my dad brings my mom flowers to mark their "monthly" anniversary. On the paper around the flowers he writes the number of months they have been married. And as far as I know, my dad has never missed a month. "Happy 435" will be what he will write this September.

Anniversaries were always a big deal for my parents, and as a child, I remember having trouble understanding the jokes I heard occasionally about the husband who forgot the anniversary. At first, I thought it meant forgetting the "monthly" anniversary, which I could almost understand. I was horrified to learn that it meant forgetting the actual yearly anniversary. In my family, that would have been unthinkable. For each anniversary, my mother would write my dad a rhyming poem detailing the events of the year. My dad would buy or make my mom something out of the official material for that year of marriage. They would always go someplace special for dinner—I knew it was fancy because my mom took her small black purse, and came home with sesame breadsticks and mints for my sister and me.

In a couple of weeks, Bill and I will celebrate our tenth year of marriage. I have decided to declare a jubilee year for our family, starting on our anniversary date. I thought the Church had an excellent idea with its Jubilee 2000 celebration, which included Masses and events throughout the year. Like the Pope, I see no reason to contain our celebrating to one day. (And like the Pope, what I declare in our family tends to come to pass, though not always without dissension.)

Why a jubilee year for a tenth anniversary? Anniversaries, much as I love them, are like Valentine's Day and New Year's Eve in terms of unrealistically high expectations for levels of fun and romance. After 10 years of marriage, romantic nights are not as easy to come by as they used to be. Especially with that crib in our room. A yearlong jubilee celebration gives Bill and me a fighting chance.

A jubilee year will be an opportunity to consciously decide to do more of those things that brought us together in the first place. At our stage of life, marriage can easily spin into rounds of the endless chores it takes to keep a family of five relatively clean, healthy and well fed. But I did not marry my husband because I loved the way he could scrape paint off an old window. And I know he did not fall in love with me because of my outstanding ability to wipe jelly off the face of a squirming toddler.

I fell in love with Bill as we ran together along the banks of the Milwaukee River. It was during these runs that we would talk about our hopes and dreams for the future. Now, because of schedules, we mostly run one at a time. During our jubilee year, I am declaring that we run together at least once or twice a week. Jacob and Liam are old enough to ride their bikes for our three-mile run and Tonisha loves her running stroller. I am hoping for some good conversation as the boys race ahead and Tonisha munches on a graham cracker.

Our jubilee year will be the chance to say "yes" more often to the best parts of marriage and family life. We love going to Lake Michigan and looking at the water as the kids try to skip rocks. We love family bike rides and morning picnics with bagels and hot coffee. We all love playing ball and Frisbee. Why don't we do these things more often? Well, there are socks to sort and the papers from the kids' school seem to breed at night and multiply if left untouched. There are big globs of blue toothpaste stuck to the side of the sink basin in the upstairs bathroom. The porch needs repainting and Liam said he saw a mouse in the garage.

It sometimes feels like if we don't keep on top of our jobs around the house, our home might actually collapse around us. I can't help but believe, however, that the same must be true of our relationship as a couple. A marriage, like a house and a yard, must be given care and time or it will start to become dilapidated. Without time together to talk, relax and have fun, Bill and I will drift apart and our family will suffer because of it.

The exchange of vows is the first hint a couple receives that marriage is not always easy. And during difficult times in our marriage, Bill and I lean on those vows. We hold onto the sacrament we received one sunny day in September ten years ago. We hold on, believing we are not together by chance, but because there are things we are called to do together that we cannot do separately.

This year, we will try to lean on the vows less and celebrate them more. And if you stop by our house and notice that the windows seem more smudged than usual and the lawn needs weeding, don't be alarmed. We will get to lawn and home maintenance eventually. But during our jubilee year, we'll do the marriage maintenance first.

❧   ❧   ❧

Loving God, thank you for the gift of my spouse.
Inspire us to take time for each other,
to rediscover what brought us together in the first place.

CHAPTER NINETEEN

Living the Vows

*F*or our tenth wedding anniversary, Bill and I got together with four of my Marquette University roommates. All five of us had gotten married between June and November of the same year. The five of us and our husbands, along with two other Marquette couples and a total of 14 children, gathered in the middle of the Marquette campus at the St. Joan of Arc Chapel for a Mass and renewal of vows.

As Marquette students, we had often attended 10 P.M. daily Mass together at the chapel. A small stone building, the chapel was built in France in the 1400s and brought to Marquette stone by stone. St. Joan of Arc has a capacity of 50 or 60, depending on how close together you sit on the wooden benches. If you are a student rushing to Mass a few minutes late from a long night studying at the library, you will sit on the stone floor.

Now, thirteen years out of college, we were back in the tiny chapel. And the theme seemed to be sippy cups.

As we prayed together, sang and broke bread, there was the constant underlying noise of small children. A book being dropped. A pacifier being thrown. A question being asked in a loud stage whisper. And occasionally, a wriggling, crying toddler who was quickly whisked outside the chapel for a few minutes.

We listened and prayed as we could, and the children participated in the liturgy as they were able. Jacob and Jeremiah, both eight, proclaimed the second reading together, and a few of the preschoolers brought up the gifts. It was not the quiet, reflective Joan of Arc Mass of our college days, nor was it nearly as formal or well-organized as our weddings. Instead, the liturgy bore witness to our mode of worship and of living right now—noisy and messy and full of interruptions, with the vows and the Eucharist in the middle of it all.

And I couldn't help but think, as I stood with my friends and made those promises to my husband once again, that we all understood so much more of what we were promising this time around. We knew about arguments and tears; about loss of jobs and late nights with sick children; we even understood more about the true duration of a lifelong promise. There were no flowing white dresses to give us the illusion that we were beginning a fairy tale. And because of these things, I believe that our 10-year anniversary vows held more weight than our original ones could have hoped for. Having experienced both the joy and the sorrow of marriage, we were coming back for more.

As our children watched, the older ones from their chairs, the younger ones in our arms, we vowed once again to be true to each other in good times and in bad, in sickness and in health; we vowed to love and honor each other all the days of our lives.

And then, our children, who somehow managed to make living those vows both more wonderful and more difficult than

I could have imagined as a young bride, clapped for us as we kissed.

⚜   ⚜   ⚜

Loving God, as loud and as messy as my life may get,
help me to keep You and my vows at the center.

CHAPTER TWENTY

Gank You Very Much

*T*onisha, our two-year-old foster daughter, is a good talker. While she came to us at 16 months with no words at all, she now makes up for that initial silence with a steady stream of comments about the world around her. She can name body parts and household objects, family members and favorite foods. She has even started stringing words together: "Wanna pretzel, Mom," or "I do it self."

My favorite phrase of hers, however, is "gank you." Tonisha "ganks" us for everything. Breakfast in the morning. A drink before bed. Zipping her zipper. Blowing her nose. When her brothers hand her an out-of-reach toy or help her hold a crayon, she often responds with a hearty, "Gank you, Liam" or "Gank you, Gacob."

Both Liam and Jacob—five and eight—are reasonably polite kids and usually remember their manners, but Tonisha has brought the art of thanking to a new level and often remembers when they forget. At the risk of sounding annoyingly braggy, I will state that Tonisha may be gifted at gratitude.

Tonisha's "ganking" has made me think about thankfulness more than I ever have before. And in thinking about thankfulness, I have come to a startling discovery. Thankfulness, in its deepest form, is love. Thankfulness is what makes us strong.

The other day, I was passing out pancakes to my ravenous children. They inhaled them so quickly, I could hardly finish pouring another round on the griddle before they were ready for more. As I tossed two more pancakes onto Liam's plate, he suddenly looked at me and said, "You always get your pancakes last, Mom. You give us ours first. That's generous." As I blinked my surprise, he added that "generous" was a new word for him, and wasn't I surprised he knew it? I was surprised he knew generous (or "gener-wuss" as he said it) but I was more surprised he noticed I got my pancakes last, and that he appreciated it.

Seeing gratitude in my children has made me think about my own gratitude in my relationship with God. Liam's comments made me feel proud of him—a moment of, "He gets it; he is seeing me; he's not thinking the pancakes just materialized out of nowhere." Could it be God has a similar reaction when I pray in a spirit of thanksgiving? I imagine God chuckling, "She finally understands this is not coincidence or her own doing, but rather my hand at work in her life."

Thanking another person—or thanking God—requires the thanker to spend a moment outside of himself or herself. Gratitude is recognition of the other, and we cannot recognize the other if we are too focused on ourselves.

I don't know if I demand more "pleases" or "thank you's" out of my children than does the average mother. I do know however, that those words were drilled into me at an early age and when I became a parent myself, I passed on the tradition. It made sense to me that if being a child means you get your cereal poured for you, your shoes tied, and (if you're lucky) cookies baked and given to you warm and gooey with a glass of cold milk, the least you can do is say "thanks."

By teaching children to be thankful, we are giving them a lifetime gift. The exact opposite of being a thankful person is being a complainer, and as far as I can tell, complainers have awful lives. For a complainer, nothing is cooked well enough in restaurants or arranged conveniently enough in stores. Everything about their jobs, families and relationships is a difficult trial.

While we all have legitimate complaints at times, I would never want one of my children to grow up with an attitude focused on the negative. The best way to make sure my children find joy in their adult lives is to teach them to be thankful as children. Thankfulness, when learned young, becomes a habit and a vantage point.

A spirit of thankfulness will make my children stronger. They will be better able to look outside themselves and serve those people who truly do not have as much to be thankful for. They will have fuller relationships, because they will be accustomed to looking for the gift—not the flaw—in their neighbor.

In our family, only three of the five of us have mastered the "th" sound. But that will not stop us from giving thanks this year. Whether it's Tonisha's "ganks" or Liam's "sanks," we're a pretty grateful bunch. And I'm thankful for that.

❦   ❦   ❦

Loving God, help me retain a spirit of gratitude.

CHAPTER TWENTY-ONE

Magic of Five

*T*oday, I was unloading groceries from the car, and Liam was helping. He came into the kitchen as I was stuffing bags of frozen vegetables into the freezer. Two boxes of Cheerios were clasped tightly in his arms and his face was radiant.

"Cheerios!" He was beside himself with his good fortune. Just this morning, he had been wishing we had Cheerios, and now, here they were. As he continued unpacking the groceries, he shouted out the name of each food item, followed by the name of the family member most likely to appreciate it.

"Half and half! Mom! For your coffee! Wow! I'll let you put that away. I know you love it. Jacob! Crackers! Here you go! And bananas! We all love bananas!"

Living with five-year-old Liam is like living with a human shot of espresso. You wouldn't think someone so small would have quite so many opinions and approach all of them with such passion.

Five is a magical age. Anything is possible for a five-year-old and those of us lucky enough to live with one should soak up the magic while we can.

"I believe this might be the fossil of a button," Liam

announced earlier this afternoon, examining a small bit of plastic he found attached to the couch. Actually, it was a hardened dot of glue that had dripped from my hot glue gun, but I didn't have the heart to tell him. A fossil of a button sounded mysterious and scientific, two attributes I had never before associated with our family room couch.

Liam and his kindergarten classmates are newly hatched in the world of childhood. Four-year-olds are still shaking off the last residue of babyhood, but five-year-olds have been in the "big kid" camp for a full year, and the result is bold confidence. They have mastered eating with a fork, doorknobs, and printing their names. What else is there?

Five-year-olds live in a place where God and the Tooth Fairy exist in harmony, and communication with either is easy and direct.

"When we go to Florida, we will leave a map for the Easter Bunny," Liam informed me shortly after I told him of our family's plan for spring break.

Liam's teacher has been teaching five-year-olds for 20 years and is unapologetic about her bias toward them.

"I teach the best age," she says every year at the kindergarten open house. "Some days I can't believe I get paid for this." Parents who stop by for an afternoon of volunteering don't think she could possibly be paid enough.

"It's like herding cats," an exhausted mom told me after an afternoon of helping.

Tuesdays, Liam goes to my parents' home in the morning while I work. My dad started teaching him to play poker a few months ago, and he has caught on pretty quickly. When my sister visited recently, she and her husband sat down for a game of poker with pajama-clad Liam and Jacob before the boys went to bed. After Liam was down for the night, my sister told me there was something strange about hearing him say, "Deuces are wild," and noting the rustle of his Pull-up at the same time.

To me, that statement summarizes Liam—and five-year-olds in general. They can play poker, but they may wear a Pull-up to bed. They are learning to read, but Teletubbies still has a hold on them. They can talk and reason, but they aren't beyond slipping to the floor in a wailing mess of a non-verbal tantrum.

Five-year-olds straddle two worlds. Time and space are liquid. To a five-year-old, there isn't too much difference between six days and six months. Both are impossibly far off. Chicago and Tokyo are equal as possible travel destinations.

Self-consciousness is still evolving. One day, Liam is horrified to be seen in his underwear by his two-year-old sister, but the next, I will find him on his bedroom floor, naked, pushing a hot wheels car down a ramp, having forgotten he was in the middle of getting dressed.

I am not sure I saw the magic of five as much with Jacob. Jacob, at five, seemed old to me. At the time, I could not foresee how different middle childhood is from early childhood. I didn't anticipate the sudden jump in knowledge and understanding. I didn't know that the magic begins to fade as early as first grade.

But I know it now. And while it is always a pleasure talking to 8-year-old Jacob, firmly rooted in reality, I am enjoying the fossils of buttons and the maps for the Easter Bunny while they still exist.

✸   ✸   ✸

I give thanks for bananas, for half and half, for Cheerios and the wonder of everyday life.

CHAPTER TWENTY-TWO

Property Taxes and Catholic School

"Why do you send your boys to a Catholic school?" my sons' pediatrician asked, at our visit last week, looking at the St. Monica school sweatshirts and uniform pants my two boys had strewn over the floor of the examining room. It was the boys' yearly check-up, and they sat expectantly in their Hot Wheels underwear as their doctor walked in.

"You live in one of the top school districts in the state," the doctor continued, taking out an instrument and peering into Liam's ear. "You're paying for those schools with your taxes. You should be taking advantage of them." He tapped Liam on the knee with a tiny hammer and Liam's eyes widened as his leg shot up in reflex.

One of the reasons I like my sons' pediatrician is that he is not afraid to challenge me. Whether he is trying to convince me to buy more organic produce or switch the boys from regular milk to soy milk, the doctor has an opinion on everything, and I always leave his office with something to think about.

As the doctor finished with Liam and moved onto Jacob, I explained to him that while my husband and I have great respect for the public schools in our area, we want our boys to learn about their faith on a daily basis.

"But you can teach them that at home," the doctor said. "Save your tuition money."

At home. I don't know how other people's homes function, but to match St. Monica's 45 minutes of daily religious instruction would be a stretch in our household where some days we don't have an extra 45 seconds to find a matching pair of socks.

But even more than the daily religion classes, there are a thousand tiny things that happen over the course of a year at a Catholic school—things I would simply have to give up if we chose public education over Catholic.

If we chose a public school, I could maybe commit to pray more with my boys at home, but I still would not be able to give them the prayer experience of 20 children and a teacher gathered in a circle, reading from a Children's Bible. And our prayers together would not be nearly as age-appropriate—I wouldn't know where to begin looking for all the cute hand-motion prayers and Jesus songs they have been taught over the past few years. I doubt that I would find the energy to have the boys make their own Advent wreaths or draw Stations of the Cross booklets for Lent.

A couple of weeks ago, I was packing Jacob's lunch in the morning, and I asked him if they pray before lunch at school.

"Of course," Jacob said, looking at me as if I had asked him if they use pencils in second grade. Not wanting to be out-done, Liam pointed out that the kindergartners pray before snack, since they don't stay for lunch.

If we chose a public school, we would need to give up the Wednesday morning all-school Masses, where some days, the

same boys Jacob plays football with at recess are that morning's readers. Where his babysitter might be one of the eighth
graders bringing up the gifts. Where kids from his school bus
are singing in the choir. If we chose a public school, we would
give up the one homily per week that is aimed at our children—homilies that include such things as what Jesus says
about how to treat your friends or how to act toward your
brother or sister.

A public school could possibly mean teachers who have
bigger budgets for classroom supplies, but it would also mean
passing up the opportunity to have Christian values blended
into all subjects—hitting would be against the school rules,
but the Golden Rule could not be brought into the discussion.
Liam's kindergarten teacher could not call her science lessons
"Learning About God's Wonderful World" and Jacob would
not be writing Bible verses for handwriting practice. As my
boys grow, they could not discuss serious social studies topics
such as war, poverty, racism and terrorism within the context
of how we are called to respond as Christians.

The thousand reasons that add up to a rationale to pay both
property taxes and Catholic school tuition are as small as a
whispered prayer before a test and as large as the bronze cru-
cifix hanging on the outside wall of the school, near the playground. The reasons are as varied as the different languages,
cultures and backgrounds of the Saints our boys learn about
in school. The thousand reasons for choosing a Catholic
school are imperfect—as imperfect as the people of God who
make up the school. Some of our reasons are not reasons at all,
but rather questions—questions about faith and life and God
that my husband and I have not figured out yet—questions a
Catholic school cannot answer, but only honor.

Somehow, I believe that my sons' Catholic school tuition is indeed a property tax.

Ultimately, my boys are property of God. It is a tax I will gladly pay.

❧ ❧ ❧

Loving God, I am not the only one sharing my faith with my children. Be with the others.

CHAPTER TWENTY-THREE

God in School

*I*t is hard to walk more than ten feet in our sons' school, St. Monica, without seeing a wall hanging, bulletin board, statue or class project that has to do with some aspect of God, faith or values. Some might see this as a lack of subtlety, but I like it. While I have great respect for the public schools in our neighborhood, we went with a Catholic school because of the faith component.

If St. Monica School chooses to barrage my children with construction-paper Gospel quotes, glossy inspirational posters, and crucifixes at every turn, I am not going to complain. When they are not in school, McDonald's is doing the same thing with ads for super-sized fries.

Every time third-grade Jacob comes in for recess, he sees this year's theme — "God has chosen you," hanging in the hall near the drinking fountain. Liam needs to walk past a bulletin board with a Psalm on it on his way to his kindergarten classroom. Granted, he may only be able to read the high-frequency words in that Psalm, but still, I like it. I am glad Saint Monica herself and her three children stand guard in a beautiful oil painting outside the office, and a statue of the child Jesus watches over the children as they go up and down the stairs.

St. Monica is not unique among religious schools in its commitment to adorning hallways and classrooms with sacred words and images. I have taught in two Catholic schools and visited many others—of all different faiths, and while each school has its own style, they hold in common an understanding that if faith is to be part of children's school day, expressions of that faith must be all around them.

A sixth grade teacher at St. Monica put it this way: "The spiritual component of St. Monica is like air inside of a balloon. It's what's filling up the school." While the teacher was speaking specifically of St. Monica, I believe the same can be said for any faith-based elementary school, high school or university that does its job well.

I see the "air in the balloon" analogy so clearly when my sons have their friends over. As I drive kids home after a play date, talk invariably turns to school. Mixed in with conversations about who scored the most touchdowns at recess are offhanded remarks that I would not hear if they went to a public school. Sentences that start, "Yesterday, after church, we . . ." or "For Advent, our class is . . ."

Before Christmas, Jacob and his friend Joe used the ride home to practice for their upcoming Christmas concert. They were belting out "I Saw Three Ships Come Sailing In" with an energy particular to eight-year-old boys. As they bellowed "the Virgin Mary and Christ were there, on Christmas Day, on Christmas Day" I glanced in the rearview mirror and couldn't help but think that we already got our money's worth out of our tuition payment, and the year was only half over.

I think faith-based schools do their job so well in terms of faith formation that they raise the bar for us as parents. If St. Monica School hands our sons Christianity neatly wrapped up in religion assignments, prayer services and paintings of Saints, it is up to us to unwrap that Christianity at home. When Christianity is unwrapped, though, it gets messy. And the closer you follow Jesus, the messier it can get. The areas Christ chooses to trod—where people are hungry, naked, or in prison—are rarely neat and tidy.

My husband and I once heard a great homily that included the refrain, "Come on in, the muck is fine." The priest was saying that being a follower of Jesus is not like diving into crystal clear water, it is more like wading into muck. To be a follower of Jesus is to get involved in messy situations you might rather avoid. In muck, you can't see the bottom, and you fear you might get stuck. From the shore, muck can look scary, but once you're in—once you're immersed in it—you find it is not so difficult after all, and you invite others to join you. Come on in, the muck is fine.

If St. Monica's job is to teach my boys about their faith, my charge is to help them live it. Our current family muck happens to be foster care. The children's court system is murky and little is clear about our foster daughter's future. From the boys' point of view, Tonisha is equal parts fun little sister and a whirling tornado who can destroy a Lego tower in one swoop. And the messiest part is yet to come—the day when Tonisha is returned to her birth family and we are left in a quieter, neater house with all Lego towers standing. And on that day, I will be so grateful to be sending our boys to a school where the spiritual component is like air in a balloon. I will be so grateful for the prayers that will surround my sons.

❧ ❧ ❧

May we have the courage to say,
"Come on in, the muck is fine."
And may we have the courage to wade into the muck,
when someone else calls us.

CHAPTER TWENTY-FOUR

Giving Up Tonisha for Lent

*O*ur foster daughter Tonisha has been with us for 13 months, and over the course of her year with us, her birth father has fulfilled the conditions the court set for him to take custody of his daughter. The planned unification date is in a month and between now and then, Tonisha will spend more and more time with her father, beginning with overnight visits, working up to weekends, then three- and four-day visits.

Our family is giving up Tonisha for Lent.

I have never loved Lent. I have respected it as a necessary season of the Church, and I have valued it as an opportunity to discover the areas of my life that I need to die to, in order to more fully live. But I have never looked forward to it. And this year, as I page through the calendar and anticipate saying goodbye to a little girl I have come to love and laugh at and wipe the nose of, Lent looms like an unwelcome desert.

I don't know the faith of Tonisha's father, or even if he has a faith, but I know our family's time of loss and pain will be his family's Resurrection. Tonisha has never lived with her father, so her going to him will be a rebirth for her. Her two full brothers, ages three and four, already live with him, and they too will receive the gift that is Tonisha, a gift that we must help our own sons to give away.

The other day, Tonisha's father called, and as we chatted, he told me he had never seen a young child run with such speed.

"She is going to be a track star someday," he said. "I'm going to need to train her in track and field."

I told him I agreed, that I had seen the potential too. But I didn't tell him that I had once been a track star myself, and up until the last court hearing, a part of me hoped maybe, just maybe, we would keep her and I would turn her into the fastest girl Wisconsin had ever seen.

The hardest thing about letting Tonisha go is the not knowing. I have never been to her father's home; I don't really know him; I don't know the woman he lives with or the other children in the household. And yet I know Tonisha intimately. I know she loves to wash her doll's hair in the tub, but screams when she needs to get her own hair washed. I know she gobbles up mashed potatoes, but doesn't have much use for lettuce; that it is best to let her brush her teeth by herself for a couple minutes before coming in to "check" them.

There is no way to deal with this not knowing than to simply live with it. I have read and learned too much about why children end up in foster care to naively believe everything will be perfect in her father's home. Yet, I believe enough in Tonisha's social worker and her guardian *ad litem* to accept that they would not have recommended placement with her father if it were not in Tonisha's best interest.

So I enter Lent with the understanding that from where I stand, I cannot see the whole picture. Tonisha's year with us is a small slice of who she is, and who she will someday become. I enter Lent believing that God's plans for Tonisha are bigger than Bill and me and our boys. Good Friday always comes before Easter Sunday. And what the disciples saw as the end turned out to be just the beginning.

ଚ   ଚ   ଚ

Loving God, I don't know the why's and the where's of your plan.
Give me the courage to follow you even when
I don't know where You are leading me.

CHAPTER TWENTY-FIVE

Less than Perfect

My life looks nothing like a Mother's Day ad.

Each year, around Mother's Day, the newspaper brims with glossy pages from local department stores showcasing beautiful mothers interacting quietly and peacefully with their beautiful children. The ads are often muted photographs with pastel backgrounds. Children and mothers frolic—hair flowing, sundresses blowing—amid fields of flowers. Immaculate children beam up at their mothers adoringly. Mothers throw back their heads in ecstatic laughter at the sheer joy of simply being in the presence of their obviously gifted children. And the father (fit, tan and back from his day at work as the president of a multinational corporation) is always looking on happily, as he grills, wearing a crisp sport shirt and khaki shorts.

I am not sure what I expect out of these ads. Realism? A picture of my own sticky, orange-popsicle stained children and me with bags under my eyes and a stringy ponytail? After all, these advertisers are trying to sell a product, and do they really want to remind people, on Mother's Day, of all days, what mothering is truly about?

It is no secret that motherhood suffers from romanticized images. From the time we are little girls, we have been fed a notion of motherhood that is sweet and serene and wrapped in a pink satin bow. No one mentioned to me before I became a mother, that between my own lactating and newborn Jacob's spit up, I would likely smell like sour milk by the end of each day.

It is not that I don't believe motherhood is a beautiful thing. Motherhood is filled with moments of beauty and grace. But mothers are beautiful in the way marathon runners are beautiful. They are beautiful for their power and strength and endurance.

A mother is beautiful because of the pain and effort you see etched on her face when she is working her hardest. Indeed, you might not even see her during those moments she is working her hardest, because it is very dark at three in the morning, and no one is up except her and the feverish infant.

The images of perfect mothers and the pressed and starched children that we see in ads may actually undermine the very motherhood that they are trying to celebrate. They show mothering at its easiest—when everyone is well-dressed and having fun.

I have always felt that the most important work of mothering is done when my children are at their worst, rather than when they are at their best. It is easy to love and guide children when they are smiling and sitting quietly. (Quick, take a picture while you can!) It is much more difficult when they are rolling their eyes or pounding on a sibling. Yet, it is how a mother handles these times that defines and shapes her child's character.

When Liam, was three, we went through a difficult time. Whenever something didn't go his way, he would scream. No cookies before dinner. Long scream. Time to turn off the TV. Longer scream. And now let's put on your pajamas. Scream within a scream; so high-pitched you can't even hear it for the first second. That very loud period of parenting, which lasted about three or four months, taught me that you never know what you are going to be called upon to teach your child. Those months, we had to teach Liam not to scream. We did it by carrying the screaming, writhing Liam to his room for a time-out every time he screamed. Sometimes we had to hold the door shut. We were pretty successful, and today Liam seldom screams.

Teaching children to go from horrible to acceptable is not exactly the most rewarding type of teaching. Starting at acceptable and heading toward outstanding is a lot more fun. It is also rare. As a mom, often you are simply teaching someone how to be a civilized human being. You are trying to bring them up to neutral. And if for some reason you think that everyone else's kids are perfect—that other mothers don't need to teach their children which words are not allowed, or how to put their laundry in the hamper, or not to scream incessantly—you could feel pretty bad about your own situation. My friend is currently trying to teach her toddler not to lick all flat surfaces. Again, just up to neutral.

Our church sometimes adds to the myth of perfect mother, perfect child. Statues and paintings of Mary—our ultimate role model—never show her in the midst of dealing with toddler Jesus in a meltdown. Yet, Jesus, arguably the best sharer of all time, once had to be taught to share himself. And Mary, perhaps exasperated after an afternoon of watching little John the Baptist and Jesus together while her cousin ran errands, was his likeliest teacher.

It can be tempting to pretend to be that perfect mom with the perfect kids in the ad; to pretend to be that serene Mother Mary. With the right outfit and a pasted-on smile, no one has to know that your kids aren't perfect. But I believe that when we look at a child struggling with a particular behavior, we need to keep in mind that there are adults with that same problem (in Liam's case, I thought of temper-losing grown-ups). And if we can help our child move beyond lying or cheating at 6 or 10 or 15, we have given that child a gift much greater than we would have if we pretended everything was just fine.

Glossy ads and marble statues aside, on Mother's Day, may we honor all not-perfect mothers and our not-perfect children. May we honor the marathon that is motherhood—often exhausting and frustrating, yet somehow exhilarating. And when we see a struggling mother, may we offer her a sip of cool water and a moment of rest. And remind her how far she has come.

❧   ❧   ❧

Loving God, I offer you my struggles and my frustration.
Help me to remember that from difficulty comes growth.

PART III:

*We Feed Them and
They Just Keep Growing*

CHAPTER TWENTY-SIX

The Second Floor

$\mathcal{J}$acob is on the second floor of his school this year. Fourth grade. Twenty-two steps above the primary grades. Not on the same floor as the kindergartners anymore. He is on a different level now, both literally and figuratively. Fourth grade is the beginning of the intermediate grades. Intermediate—in the middle. Jacob and his classmates are in the middle of childhood. Nine years old, they are halfway to 18. Halfway through grade school.

And while I understand the whole point of parenthood is to help your child grow and develop—I am still getting used to being the mom of a larger-sized kid. Jacob's clothes aren't cute and tiny anymore and haven't been for some time. I could wear his t-shirts if I wanted. (Yes, if I wanted to constantly walk around with large numbers on my back and chest.) If his feet continue to grow at their current rate, I should be able to fit into his shoes in a few months. Already, I have mistaken his black dress pants for cropped pants of my own; I hung them in my closet and only realized my error when I began to put them on and they stopped suddenly at my hips.

Jacob is still a good ten inches shorter than I am, and easily forty pounds lighter, but my days of being the expert at everything are clearly numbered. This summer, I had to admit that he is better than I in baseball. If I were to be completely honest, I would acknowledge this might have been true as many as two years ago, and quite certainly one, but this summer was the first summer I thought about it.

We went to a park one afternoon, and I stood on the pitcher's mound, Jacob's sometime-position in little league, and I pitched to him. It looked so easy when I watched him from the stands, but as I struggled to get the ball over the plate, I apologized to my son for making him wait so long for a decent pitch.

"That's okay, Mom," he said. "You pitch pretty well, for a writer."

My child was giving me qualified encouragement that I was doing okay. I wasn't doing as well as he, of course—who would expect that? He wore the numbers. He was the baseball player. I was the mom. And the writer.

And though I knew Jacob's assessment of the situation was accurate, somehow in my mind, it wasn't possible that Jacob could be better at baseball than me—after all, I was the one who taught him how to hold a bat in the first place. I was the one who pitched the enormous white whiffle ball directly at his fat red bat when he was a toddler, willing the ball to stop in mid-air so he could make contact. I called it a hit, even when it would more accurately be called a pitch that tapped the bat. And now he is better than me. Much better.

I told my friend Eric, who has a two-year-old, that the day is coming when his daughter will be better than he at something.

"It's already here," he said. "She can dance better. She has more rhythm."

I look at Jacob and know baseball is just the beginning of a long list of things he will one day do better than I. If early childhood was for learning basic skills, middle childhood is for refining those skills. And while one side of my heart cheers wildly for Jacob as he conquers long division, the strike zone, and increasingly adult-looking novels, the other side of my heart wants to freeze time. For the middle of childhood—age nine—is so clearly the beginning of something big. And I have learned from babyhood on that beginnings are fleeting. I am afraid that middles may be fleeting, too.

He is on the second floor this year. Halfway through grade school. Halfway through childhood. A tall, skinny kid with a huge appetite, a big smile and talents neither of us knows about yet.

I'm running to keep up.

❧   ❧   ❧

Loving God, time moves so quickly.
Give me the grace to change and grow with my children;
to rejoice in their new abilities.

CHAPTER TWENTY-SEVEN

Shelter from the Storm

Tonisha has been gone six months now.

Throughout Tonisha's year with us, one of the comments Bill and I heard a lot was, "I could never be a foster parent. I couldn't give them back."

But when you are a foster parent, giving them back is part of the deal. In some ways, being a foster parent is like being a tornado shelter. When the storm is over, you come out of your shelter, spend a great deal of time cleaning and rebuilding, and then resume your life. To wish a child could stay is tantamount to wishing the his or her family's storm—be it alcohol abuse, drug addiction or one of the many other effects of poverty—will level the original family, destroy it, make it unlivable. It happens, yes, but you don't wish for it. In Milwaukee County, three of four foster children are returned to either a rehabilitated birth parent or a willing relative. The others, whose parents' rights are terminated, are adopted by their foster family or another family.

Giving them back is part of the deal.

Tonisha's birth father chose to sever contact with us after she was returned to him and we have not seen her since. The most difficult part, for me, seems to be over now. I think about her in little ways; when I find a marble on the floor and remember how I was always sweeping her mouth to check for small toys. Sometimes one of her socks shows up in the wash. I never know how it gets there, but then, the where and when of socks and laundry are a great mystery to me. We have photos of her mixed in with pictures of the boys, on the wall and in albums.

Bill and I both dream about her. Scary, searching dreams where we are frantically looking for Tonisha, who is inexplicably lost. Somehow, in the dreams, we never remember she was returned to her father.

I often think of her when I go for my daily run through a nearby park. Our neighborhood, just east of the park, is mostly white; the neighborhood just west of the park is mostly black.

Running in the park reminds me that too often, skin color is an "either" rather than a "both." Either you are white and you live and play here, or you are black and you live and play there. The park is a reminder that Tonisha, who is black, might not have had it easy in our white family, much as we loved her and she loved us. I know the family life she has been returned to will not be easy either, but the large family picnics I run past are a hope for me—a hope that Tonisha's family will heal to the extent that someday, she will have a family celebration of her own.

The time I remember Tonisha most is during Eucharist at Mass. I never plan to see her then, but a memory nevertheless dashes in, a fast toddler with some place to be. I see her scribbling with a fat orange crayon during the Consecration and feel her squirming weight in my arms as I walk up to Communion. Once, during the fraction rite, as the priest was pouring wine into four glasses, it reminded me of how many times the past year I poured juice for three kids, and now I pour for two. Our family fraction rite has changed. My boys are so used to seeing me cry during the Eucharist that I sometimes notice them peering over as we kneel, to see if I have started yet. We smile at each other in recognition of the strange, new ritual.

But from my vantage point of six months after Tonisha, I can honestly say that the joy of having had her far outweighs the hurt of having lost her. Six months after her leaving, we have been assured by her social worker that her family situation is stable enough that she is unlikely to bounce back into the foster care system. Knowing we are not needed for Tonisha anymore, we are once again ready to put our name on the list to accept another foster child. We don't know who that child is, but many nights at dinner, our boys pray for that child after they pray for Tonisha.

"Bless Tonisha and bless whoever we're going to get next," one of them will say.

It is not a prayer for tornadoes, but a prayer of recognition that tornadoes exist.

We are readying our shelter. Wondering if our shelter will be a temporary haven or a permanent home. And as we get ready, we are remembering Tonisha, knowing somehow, a part of her will join us in welcoming this new child.

℘   ℘   ℘

Loving God, I bring to mind someone
who is no longer a part of my daily life,
but whom I still love. Bless this person.

CHAPTER TWENTY-EIGHT

Not Believing in Coincidence

I met my husband because of a spinning pencil.

Bill was 22, a new college graduate recently moved back to Milwaukee. After a summer of living with his parents, a buddy convinced him it was time to move out. The pages of apartment rentals in the Sunday paper seemed daunting to the guys, so Bill spun a pencil and announced that wherever it ended up pointing to, they would live.

The point stopped on an ad for the apartment across the hall from where my college roommate and I had just signed a lease.

Meetings and beginnings are fascinating to me. Looking back on Bill and me moving in across from one another, I know now that there could not have been a better way that we could have met and started dating. I got to know Bill as we picked up our mail together; as we talked in the hall with our keys in the locks, not opening our doors. I took note of the environmental posters and the cross on his living room wall. He was glad to see I had a high-quality bicycle. Bill's subtle humor and thoughtful personality came through quietly and gradually. If I had instead met him while out with friends, I might not have slowed down enough to learn who he was.

Thirteen years, one marriage, two sons and three foster children later, I think about the Holy Spirit present in that pencil spin. While I am cautious about using the phrase, "It was meant to be," I do believe God offers us opportunities through the people we come in contact with. God nudges us to meet those who could help us grow and learn or who could benefit from something we might be able to teach. Whether we seize the opportunity or not is where free will comes in. Yet, even as I hesitate to say, "It was meant to be," it seems that sometimes, it is.

We received our third foster child last week. Jamilet is 14 months old, Latina and beautiful.

Jamilet has been in foster care for over a year, since she was two days old. Social Services called us a month ago to tell us about her situation. She was with a wonderful foster family, the social worker explained, but it was now looking like there was a chance her birth parents' rights would be terminated. Because of this possibility, Jamilet needed to be moved to a foster home where the parents were open to adoption, should this become necessary. Her current foster parents were in their 50s and adopting baby Jamilet was not an option—they had grown biological children and an adopted 13-year-old. Bill and I said that we were interested and set up a time to meet.

The night before we were to meet Jamilet for the first time, I went to my monthly book club meeting.

I had not told the group about the potential foster child yet, and as we stood around drinking wine and chatting, Kris, a mom of two, turned to me and said, "I thought of you the other day. The grandmother of a girl on my son's soccer team is a foster mother, and her foster baby needs to be moved. I told

her I knew the perfect family—yours, but she said social services already picked out a family."

Something about the situation made me ask some follow-up
questions. Was the woman white? Yes. Did she have a 13-
year-old African American son? Yes. Was the baby about a
year old and of Puerto Rican descent? Yes.

In a metro area of over a million people, someone from my
eight-person book club had met our soon-to-be foster daughter—had sat next to her at soccer games—and was telling me
this twelve hours before I was due to meet her for the first
time.

"She's darling," Kris said, as we realized it had to be the
same family. "You'll love her. Her foster mother's name is
Judy."

Over the past month, as we have transitioned Jamilet to
our home, there have been other profound coincidences—
spinning pencil moments—that have made Bill and me pause.

Judy's best friend, another foster mom, turns out to be the
foster mother Bill and I invited over three years ago when we
were first considering foster care—we had received her name
from a friend of a friend. Listening to her story inspired us to
sign up for the certification classes. We had not seen her since,
but Judy sees her a few times a week.

Jamilet's physical therapist, we learned, is Julie, a good
friend of mine from college. Julie was working with Jamilet
one week, and when she heard the description of the family
Jamilet would be moving to, she recognized it as ours.

Jamilet shares a birth date with my friend's brother who
recently died unexpectedly.

Judy told me her pastor does not believe in coincidences—
he calls them God-incidences, or incidences of God. My friend

Amy calls them signs, and says once you start looking for them, they are everywhere.

To me, they will always be spinning pencil moments. A flash of the divine in the ordinary. A whisper from God, who is standing closer to us than we dare to hope; closer than we have the courage to believe. Spinning pencil moments. Not lightning bolts or thunder claps, just quiet reminders that the grace of God is here. Is everywhere. Welcome Jamilet.

❧　❧　❧

Loving God, help me to recognize You in the coincidences in my life. Gift me with the courage to believe that if it seems unbelievable, it is probably You at work.

CHAPTER TWENTY-NINE

Degree of Difficulty

I am fascinated by the sports of gymnastics and figure skating. It is not because I have any background in these areas. I could never do the straddle roll to pass beginning gymnastics, and my favorite part of ice skating is the hot cocoa afterwards. In spite of my limited talents—or perhaps because of them—I love to watch athletes defy gravity and leap, spin and flip their way to the awards podium.

I can't say I completely understand the scoring in either of these sports, but I do understand the oft-used phrase, "degree of difficulty." The more complicated a routine is, the higher the possible score the athlete can get if he or she does it perfectly.

I have decided we need to apply this phrase to parenting. Every child equals one point, or one degree of difficulty. Two additional points are awarded for each child age four and under. Parenting while pregnant earns an additional point, as does parenting anyone who is not yet sleeping through the night.

Therefore, my friend Carol, who has four children—ages one, three, five and seven, is working with a degree of difficulty of eight. My own degree of difficulty, now that we have added a one-year-old foster daughter, is up to five, having been recently down to two, when we just had the boys—ages six and nine.

My friend Patty, whose five children are now between six and twelve, once had a degree of difficulty of ten, when she was pregnant in addition to having four-year-old twins, a two-year-old and a one-year-old.

I don't have preteens or teens yet, but from what I have heard, they may require an additional point of difficulty, just as the very young children do. And teenage boy drivers may add even more, just as they do to insurance premiums.

Degrees of difficulty would be helpful for two reasons. First, because they would be applied to everything a parent does, they would turn small daily successes into major triumphs. "Did you see that, ladies and gentlemen? She's going grocery shopping with her children. That's a degree of difficulty of eight, remember. Look at that. She's actually moving down the aisle. She's keeping the three-year-old away from that display of sugared cereal, and handing a cracker to the baby—all this while getting the best price on spaghetti noodles and answering the seven-year-old's questions about dinosaurs."

Degrees of difficulty would also be good because they would be a concrete way for parents to gauge when their lives would get easier. "Hmm. When the baby starts sleeping through the night and Johnny turns five, my degree of difficulty will drop by two."

I think the main reason I am in favor of degrees of difficulty, however, is that conscientious parents are often too hard on themselves. I will go over to my friend Laura's home, where there are three children six and under (degree of difficulty, seven), and she will apologize because there are toys on the floor and the kitchen is a mess. But her crazy climbing 17-month-old is alive and relatively unbruised, and so is her three-year-old, Donovan, who has been known to wander away from the house and down the street. Toys on the floor or not, we need to call it a successful morning.

Perhaps it is my contact with the foster care system that also makes me want to publicly give voice to the difficulty of parenting. I know firsthand that what most parents consider the basics—keeping their children clothed, fed and attended to, all while making a living—can be an insurmountable task for some parents. I have seen firsthand that a parent can love a child and still neglect him or her—that the all-consuming task of parenting can become downright impossible in the face of addiction. My degree of difficulty scale did not even include parenting while in poverty, parenting while living in a dangerous neighborhood or parenting while in an abusive relationship. At some point, the degree of difficulty becomes so high that some parents give up.

And if parents are the athletes, we are also the judges. We judge each other and we judge ourselves. We judge our next-door neighbor, whose degree of difficulty may be similar to our own, and we judge those who live on the other side of the tracks, who are dealing with degrees of difficulty that we cannot even imagine.

But the thing that we too often forget as we are balancing and leaping (and judging), is that parenting is not a competition. In ice-skating, athletes may not rush out onto the ice to help each other. And a gymnast certainly may not lend a supporting hand to a teammate about to fall off the beam. But parents are not bound by these rules. As we acknowledge our own degree of difficulty—and forgive ourselves for our missteps—we must simultaneously reach out to other parents. We must cheer for each other and be ready to spot without being asked. And after a fall, we must remind each other just how complicated the routine of parenting really is.

❧   ❧   ❧

Loving God, be my coach and my guide.
Be my mat when I fall.

CHAPTER THIRTY

All I Want for Christmas Is a Hyper Jet

$\mathcal{M}$y children never know what they want for Christmas. We have an old TV, with no cable and bad reception, and Bill and I limit most of the kids' viewing to public television. On the unusual occasions that the kids do get to watch commercial TV, we make them mute the commercials. Because of this, they rarely know what new toys are out, and therefore cannot ask for them.

So each year, when I ask them what they want for Christmas, they honestly have no idea and assure me they will be happy with whatever I pick out. And they always are.

It was about two weeks before Christmas this year when I remembered to make my cursory question as to what they might want for Christmas. I did not expect an answer and asked it just as they were about to leave to catch the school bus one morning.

"Anything will be fine," Jacob, nine, said.

Liam, six, hesitated.

"Well," he said. "There is this one thing I'd like. But it looks very expensive, like maybe even more than ten dollars. It's called a Hyper Jet, and it's so cool."

His speech was picking up speed, and he was beginning to wiggle up and down as if he might take off soon, just talking about the jet. He bounced from the porch to the step and back.

"The Rescue Heroes use the Hyper Jet to rescue people," he continued. "People who are in trouble—who have fallen off of cliffs or who are caught in an avalanche. It can turn from a jet to a robot and back again. It opens up and has a console inside and the front comes off and turns into something else. But it looks expensive. So tie shoes would be great, too," he said.

The bouncing slowed down a bit, and I looked at Liam. He smiled, completely sincere about the shoes. He really would not mind if I just got him the shoes. Tie shoes, not Velcro. He would understand if the Hyper Jet were too expensive, and he would be happy with shoes that had no console and could not rescue anything. And because of that, I wanted to somehow pull a Hyper Jet out of the closet and give it to him before school.

Liam ran off to the bus stop and I grabbed Jacob's elbow.

"Is this Hyper Jet a real thing?" I whispered. "How does he know about it?"

"He saw an ad in the paper," Jacob said. "He read all about it. It's real."

As the boys boarded the bus, I strapped the baby into her car seat. We were going to Toys R Us. Nine years into parenting, I had my first real request for a toy.

I found the Hyper Jet in the Rescue Hero aisle. It was everything I disliked in a toy. It was huge and plastic, with too many parts that could disengage and clog up the vacuum cleaner. It was, as Liam said, expensive—much more than ten dollars—even on sale, and it came with another large piece of plastic rescue equipment that looked like a walking helicopter with claws. Looking at the toy, I knew it was very likely that he would lose interest in this enormous flying robot vehicle within the next six months. The toy represented the very reason why Bill and I did not let the kids watch commercial TV. We did not want them to know toys like this were even within the realm of possibility.

I couldn't get it in my cart fast enough.

"Crazy in love" is a phrase that we usually apply to heartsick young couples. But every so often, it is a phrase we need to apply to parents, too. The Hyper Jet makes no sense. It sits in our family room, taking up vast amounts of space as Liam plays, content on the couch, with a Rubik's Cube. But the 30 seconds it took him to open it Christmas morning, the look of delirious joy on his face when he discovered what it was, the two hours he spent putting it together with his dad, all these are reasons why I bought the Hyper Jet.

I am crazy in love with my six-year-old, and most days, I can express that love in simple hugs, kisses and small trinkets. Every so often, though, the love seems to burst out of my heart and take on a life of its own.

Love as a Hyper Jet. Big, fast, rescuing love.

❦   ❦   ❦

Loving God, I am crazy in love, and I thank you for that.

CHAPTER THIRTY-ONE

A One-year-old (Again and Again)

*I*n the movie Groundhog Day, Bill Murray's character has to re-live February 2 again and again until he gets it right.

Our foster care experience has some similarities to Groundhog Day. We have been doing foster care for two years, and in that time, we have had three baby girls—all of whom have come to us at exactly 14 months. We did not request 14-month-old girls; on our foster care form, we noted we would be open to any child, age three and under.

Despite this, every time a new social worker comes to our door, she is holding a toddler girl for us.

Having gone through every parenting stage from birth to ten, it is my opinion that the year between one and two is the hardest. One-year-olds, cute as they may be, are insane. One-year-olds are a terrifying combination of total mobility and a tiny brain. I realize this was also an issue for the Tyrannosaurus Rex, and there are important similarities between the two, not the smallest of which is destructive potential. Parents of one-year-olds spend much of their time bent in half, running after their toddler, trying to prevent a calamity. Bill and I have now been doing this for two years straight.

Jamilet, our current one-year-old, is obsessed with the toilet. We must keep the lids down and the bathroom doors shut at all times. If we forget, no matter where Jamilet is in the house, some sort of toilet alert goes off in her brain, and she is off and running toward the toilet. Upon reaching the toilet, she will take any object she happens to be carrying and fling it in.

Complicating the issue is Liam, six, whose own relationship with the bathroom has always been volatile. Liam waits until the last nanosecond to use the bathroom and then sprints to it from wherever he is. This means he often cannot even spare the time to close the door. This apparently turns Jamilet's internal bathroom alert to "high" and she is off and running to the open bathroom where there is now even more potential for fun. Liam, of course, is horrified to be seen standing at the potty by his little sister, but cannot flee the scene, so his only recourse is to yell loudly until a running, bent-in-half parent appears to whisk Jamilet away. And that is just one three-minute period of the day.

As toddlers, all of our children would try to take our food. It is impossible to eat near a toddler without having the child make a grab for whatever you happen to be eating. This leaves the parent in a quandary. Do you give in, break off a bite of the food, and give it to the child, thus teaching the child to continue to grab for food whenever he or she wants, or do you say something like, "No, this is mine, you have your own cracker," and risk the high pitched screams of frustration that will follow? The year between one and two is when most women lose the remainder of the weight gained during pregnancy. This is probably because they are giving their food away, but it could also be from time they spend running around, bent in half.

Three foster one-year-olds in a row, in addition to our two boys' time as toddlers, have convinced me they all have the same agenda. I can almost imagine a boardroom meeting of one-year-olds (three of them crawling on the table, two pulling on the curtains, one crumpling papers), led by a just turned-two-year-old. The two-year-old would have a flip chart with a list of assignments for the one-year-olds. Cabinets at floor level? Open them and start to empty as fast as you can. You have been brought outside? Run toward the street. If no street, open water will do. Closets? Walk in and see what you can find. Food on the floor? Eat immediately. In fact, assume any small object on the floor is a piece of food. Done with your oatmeal? Start rubbing it on your face. If no one notices, move on to your hair. Socks? Who needs socks? Take them off. Right away.

As I write this, Jamilet is busily taking apart a ballpoint pen on the floor next to me. She has no socks on and I know that I have approximately sixty seconds to finish writing this before she toddles over to the computer tower and starts randomly pressing buttons.

But she has these enormous brown eyes, unbelievably soft skin and legs that are still a little bowed from her time in the womb. She babbles in a soft baby language and when she hugs me, it is with her whole body.

She is one, and she is crazy and sometimes my life is Groundhog Day because I am on my fifth one-year-old. But other times I think, how lucky I am that I keep catching these girls as they tumble over the threshold between infancy and childhood. Wriggling, pot-bellied little girls, bursting into my life and toddling into my heart. How lucky I am.

Except for that toothbrush in the toilet.

⚬   ⚬   ⚬

Loving God, give me the grace to see that
this stage will not last forever —
to appreciate this moment for what it offers.

CHAPTER THIRTY-TWO

My (Almost) Ashless Wednesday

I hurried to Ash Wednesday Mass across the slushy mess of the church parking lot, carrying 18-month-old Jamilet. Repositioning the diaper bag on my shoulder, I mentally checked off the things I had packed that I hoped would buy me 20 minutes of quiet time from my toddler. Twenty minutes — that is all I really needed — enough time to get through the readings, the homily and the ashes. The rest of Mass, I knew from experience, I could kind of absorb while chasing after Jamilet in the back of church, but if I missed the readings and the homily, I had nothing. Readings, homily and ashes — those were my goals for the Mass. I wanted to start Lent off right.

Lately, I had been feeling like my spirituality was withering a bit. The winter cold and mounds of snow were providing an excellent excuse to skip my daily run, which often was my best time to pray. I had a huge overdue fine on my library card (*Tarzan* had been lost for over a month) and rather than pay it I was spending my usual reading time at night watching TV, and I knew my brain was turning to mush. In addition, my husband Bill and I were struggling to find time for uninter-rupted conversations about anything deeper than whether or not to paint the back hallway. So here I was, on Ash Wednesday, putting my hopes for spiritual rejuvenation in a baggie of graham crackers, four board books, a doll with a working zipper on her dress, goldfish crackers, and the big prize—a Tootsie Roll sucker. I prayed it would be enough to keep Jamilet still.

I slunk into a pew next to my good friend, a mom attend-ing Mass child-free because her youngest was in third grade. She shared her songbook with me as I concentrated on imme-diately giving Jamilet a graham cracker so she would be busy right off the bat. I glanced at my friend, and thought I glimpsed serenity in her eyes. Having your youngest old enough to put on her own shoes could lead to serenity.

I don't know if it was my friend's air of calm rubbing off, or if I finally happened upon the right combination of food and interesting books to keep Jamilet occupied, but whatever the reason, my normally super-active little girl stayed settled and content on my lap. The readings were strong, the homily was inspiring, and it felt like a new beginning. The priest com-pared us to batteries, and said that Lent provides an opportu-nity for the positive and the negative to come together—the positive being the good we try to do during Lent, and the neg-ative, the bad habits we try to curtail. A car needs both to run properly, and so do we.

As the homily ended, Jamilet started to get restless, and I brought her to the vestibule, where four or five other mothers were standing in a cluster, watching their toddlers run. Perfect, I thought. I would let Jamilet burn some energy while the congregation went up to get their ashes, then I would jump in line at the end. Readings, homily, ashes. I was almost home free.

Except I missed the ashes.

I am still not sure how it happened. I chatted quietly for a few minutes (wasn't it just a few?) with another mom of a toddler. I put everything back in the lost-and-found box after Jamilet emptied it. I distracted her with the Tootsie Roll sucker when she tried to bang on the glass door leading to the school. But then, when I peeked back into the church, to check where the line was for receiving ashes, I was appalled to see the final two people receiving their ashes from the second grade teacher. How did I not notice the other mothers, one by one, leaving the vestibule to get in line? I briefly considered running for it, a mad dash for ashes with Jamilet on my hip, but this seemed to lack a certain solemnity, so I decided against it.

The rest of Mass was a bit of a blur. I went back to my pew, where Jamilet remained relatively quiet. Going up to Communion, I could not help but note the black mark on every person's forehead. Everyone managed to get themselves to the front of church for their ashes. Everyone but me. What did that say about me? Yes, I had listened to the readings, the Gospel, even the homily. But I had missed the ashes. I had missed the main event. I was annoyed at myself, annoyed at Jamilet, and slightly bewildered about my strong feelings about a small black mark that I knew was just a symbol.

After Mass, my dad came up to me. We had arranged to meet at Mass, so he could take Jamilet home and baby-sit while I went to work. He was putting on his baseball cap and making a silly face at Jamilet as he walked over to join us.

"I missed the ashes," I said.

"You did?" He looked at Jamilet, laughed and poked her in the tummy with his index finger. Then, he took his thumb, rubbed it on his own ashes, and traced a cross on my forehead.

"Have some of mine," he said.

❦   ❦   ❦

I give thanks that God's grace may be so easily shared.

CHAPTER THIRTY-THREE

Termination

*T*he parental rights of our foster daughter's biological parents have been terminated. "Terminate" is a terrible word. Pregnancies are terminated. Jobs are terminated. There is no going back from terminated. No second chance. No changing your mind. And much as I know that Jamilet's parents are in no position to care for her, it was still difficult to hear the Court terminate their rights. I was thankful they were not present to hear it, too. I was also thankful that one-year-old Jamilet will have no memory of this day. She will never hear the social worker, under oath, answer "No," to the ten questions the court posed regarding whether her biological parents ever provided the most basic of care. Jamilet has been in foster care since birth, and her biological mother visited her just a few times before disappearing. It is completely appropriate that the Court terminated her mother's rights. But appropriate does not make it any less heartbreaking.

Jamilet knows nothing of this. Nothing was terminated about her day-to-day life. She yells, "Daddy!" when Bill walks in the door. Often, her first word upon waking up from a nap is "IAMMM!" She cannot make the "L" sound for "Liam," so she just leaves it out entirely. When Jacob comes home from school, she holds up her arms so he can pick her up. I have learned to walk rather effectively with a small body wrapped around my leg, giggling. Jamilet is so much a part of our family that it is hard to imagine that she had her start outside of us.

But she did have her start outside us. About six weeks into Jamilet's stay with us, when she was 15 months old, our social worker set up a meeting with five of her six biological siblings at Chuck E. Cheese. All of the children in the family are in foster care or live with their respective biological fathers, but none live with their mother. We have photos and a video of that meeting. Jamilet's older sister gave me pictures of their biological mother and grandmother. More than anything, it is that day that I was thinking of in court, when Jamilet's parents' rights were terminated. The reality of day-to-day family life and complications of siblings living with so many different families, mean Jamilet will never know them well as a child. The termination of Jamilet's parents' rights, is also a de facto termination of a relationship with her biological siblings—a termination of a sisterhood with three girls who have her beautiful black curly hair and three brothers who have the same enormous brown eyes.

When Tonisha left us, I recognized in her leaving that while I could be happy that she was reunited with her birth family, I could be sad for our loss. At the time, my pain was deep and I thought that if I should ever some day be in a position to adopt a foster child, I would feel nothing but joy. As we prepare to adopt Jamilet next month, I know now that is not the case. Joy I feel, definitely, joy. But also within that joy, a tinge of sadness, for a family that could have been.

❡   ❡   ❡

Loving God, the sadness at the edge of my joy, I offer to you.

CHAPTER THIRTY-FOUR

ZIP Code Theology

Z IP codes are on my mind. My husband and I are in the beginning stages of house-hunting. With all three kids in one bedroom (sharing a closet), things in our current home are feeling a bit tight. Since right now, our lives center around the kids' school, we want to buy a house within a reasonable radius of that school. Four different suburbs surround St. Monica, but they share one ZIP code, so when I search one of the Realty web sites for houses, I enter that ZIP code as a way of narrowing the search.

Entering the ZIP code makes me a little uncomfortable because of a homily I heard a few years ago. The homily was so right on and true that it has stayed with me. I attended Mass that day with some friends, so we all heard it, and to this day, we refer to the homily as "Luck of the ZIP code."

The priest's point was that many of the successes we congratulate ourselves for, are not really ours alone, but are ours by virtue of being born into the "right" ZIP code. Strong school systems, crime-free neighborhoods and intact families are all more common in some ZIP codes than others. People who grow up in these ZIP codes have an immediate advantage over their counterparts who are born into poor, crime-ridden ZIP codes. Father John Horan cautioned us against being judgmental toward others or puffing up with pride at our own accomplishments—had we been born into a different ZIP code, our lives could be very different.

Sometimes I think of that homily as I key in the ZIP code for the area we are interested in. No one would argue that it is not a fine ZIP code to buy a home. Houses are well-maintained, streets are quiet, children are generally well-cared for and well-educated. Property values go up each year. What bothers me is not that our family has the opportunity to purchase a home in this ZIP code; it is that other families do not have this chance. The very people who could most benefit from the quiet neighborhoods and excellent school systems of our ZIP code cannot afford to live here. Once you are born into a very poor ZIP code, your chances of ever living in a wealthy one are very slim.

And that is where the second part of the priest's homily comes in. He challenged the congregation to see the inherent injustice in the luck of the ZIP code. He called us to use our own resources, talents and time to work to make things better for those whose roll of the ZIP code dice was not as fortunate as our own.

I don't know what the Gospel was the day of that homily, but it could very well have been the parable of the Good Samaritan. When Jesus tells his followers to love their neighbor, they ask him what "neighbor" means. Jesus replies with the story of the Samaritan man. Samaria was certainly in another ZIP code, and the parable shows us how Jesus calls us to reach beyond human-made borders as a response to his command to love one another.

As Bill and I continue our house hunt, I know the message of Father John's homily will stick with me, like an itch that won't go away. And that is okay. If the role of Jesus is to comfort the afflicted and afflict the comfortable, I will admit that in my search for more closet space and another bedroom, I can use a little afflicting—especially on those days when I start thinking about a first-floor laundry room. And while originally becoming a foster parent was a way of reaching out to those from other ZIP codes, we will adopt our current foster daughter this Thursday. In four days, we won't have a foster child; we will have a daughter. And as a new family of five, we will need to find another way to reach out across the ZIP code line.

⚩   ⚩   ⚩

Loving God, help us see beyond our human-made borders to what work you would have us do across the lines.

CHAPTER THIRTY-FIVE

Adoption Day

The question I hear the most since Jamilet's adoption is, "Does it feel different?" I wish I could say it did. I wish that I had some dramatic story to tell about how, at the moment of adoption, everything changed. I never liked those questions on my birthday as a kid, either. "How does it feel to be eight?" an uncle would ask. It did not feel any different.

For me, growing to love Jamilet as a daughter began the first day I met her, as a foster daughter. Just as I did not know newborn Jacob and Liam, I did not know 1-year-old Jamilet. Yet, with all three, I felt an almost instant sense of responsibility and protectiveness. I am not a fan of babysitting for other people's children, and one of my fears before I had Jacob, and then again, before I became a foster parent for the first time, would be that I would feel about the child like I did about my friends' children—fondly, but not passionately. But with both of my biological sons, my two foster daughters, and now, with adopted Jamie, the passion kicked in right away. For me, there was something about knowing I was a child's mother—whether for a month or for a lifetime—that clicked on a sense of interest and purpose I do not feel for other children. With Jacob and

Liam, with my other two foster daughters, and now with Jamie, the passage of time deepens the love. I cannot say I love Jacob more now, at ten, than I loved him when he was two, but I can say I love him more fully now. Jacob is a more complex person now; there are more aspects to love, and as I discover those aspects, I can more fully know him as God knows him. The same is true for Liam and Jamie. As they grow into who they are, I love them more fully.

In Jamie's adoption, the court recognized officially what Bill and I had long felt. She is a member of our family. There is a bond here that cannot be broken.

On adoption day, we went to the courthouse with both sets of our parents, Bill's sister and her family, Jamie's original foster mother, and my grandmother and uncle. We brought with us a bunch of pink helium balloons, and an enormous, 20-foot long, 3 foot wide pink banner, made by Liam, proclaiming, "Happy Adoption!" in big first grade block letters. He taped it to the front of the judge's bench. I got so choked up on the first question ("Please state and spell your name") that I wasn't sure if I would be able to continue. Jamie raced around the courtroom in a pretty white dress and brand new patent leather shoes, excited that everyone she knew was all together in the same room. And after all the questions were answered and the forms were signed, the judge invited the boys up to the bench. They each got to pound the gavel and say, "This adoption is final."

Finally final. We are so thankful.

∙ ∙ ∙

I give thanks for the splendid, varied ways
we have joined together to become a family.

CHAPTER THIRTY-SIX

For Sale By Owner

We just moved. Bill and I bought our first house, on Eula Court, when Jacob was thirteen months old. He learned to walk in the dining room shortly after we moved in. Jacob is now ten. The people who owned the Eula house before us had a nine-year-old when they moved out.

"It goes so fast," Julie, the previous owner, told me at the closing. I smiled at her, not really believing. Nothing about babyhood seemed to go fast to me. At the time, I was still waiting for Jacob to start sleeping through the night. At the time, it felt like I would always be the mother of a baby. I would always be in my twenties. Thirty was still far off, and school-aged children, further still.

Shortly after we moved into Eula, I found a pair of little boy's shoes in the basement. Julie must have forgotten them. They would fit Jacob at three or four, I decided, and packed them away to save. By the time I re-discovered them, Jacob had long outgrown them. I put them aside to save for Liam, and the same thing happened. I began to understand that Julie had had a point.

Selling our Eula Court house was as much a milestone for me as any graduation ever was. While our toddler, Jamie, keeps me connected to the little-kid world I have come to know so well, Jacob is pulling me hard into the next phase of parenting. Selling our first house and moving to this one was an acknowledgement of growth. Two boys and a girl in one room was fine for awhile, but it would not have been for long. I cannot help but note that while all three of our kids learned to walk in our Eula Court house, they will likely learn to drive while living in this one. Our basement at the new house still has plenty of Fisher Price toys in it, just as our last one did, but it also has a mini-pool table and a ping-pong table that show how our children's play is changing.

While I can quickly tick off a list of things the boys learned to do in our first house—from going on the potty to long division, it is what Bill and I learned that makes me even more aware of the passage of time. Some things we learned on purpose, like when we checked out the book *How to Build a Deck* from the library, convinced that if we could read, we could build. Some things we learned by uncomfortable necessity, like when Bill suddenly lost his job, and I had to change my plan to be a stay-at-home mom and go to work full time for a while. Most things, we learned gradually. Gradually, we learned the rhythms of marriage; the endurance needed for parenthood, the ebb and the flow of life as a family—a family first of three, then four, then five. We moved into our current home knowing more than we could have imagined when we moved into our last—not just about plastering, plumbing and painting, but also about ourselves as a couple. We are quicker to laugh at ourselves than we were moving in to our first house. We are more confident in who we are as a partnership, who we are professionally, who we are as parents. We know a little more about where we are heading in life, yet we have also had enough unforeseen detours to know anything is possible—that derailment often happens when you are chugging along quickly.

Kari and Drew, the couple we sold our Eula Court home to, are so young and cute they look like they stepped off the top of a wedding cake. They are eager and excited and have a dog who loves the yard where Jacob threw a thousand football passes, where Liam spent hours making forts out of sticks, where both boys, two foster children, and then Jamie, learned the rule that no one is allowed to eat the sandbox sand, tasty as it might appear. To Drew and Kari, I am sure that our mid-thirties life with three kids, homework, soccer practice and little time to worry about the towels on the bathroom floor, seems unbelievable far-off. I didn't even try to explain that it is closer than they might think.

Over the summer, as I waited for the closing dates for the two homes, I was torn between peering ahead and glancing back. I sat on my Eula Court porch and drank in the memories of our first home—the chubby baby knees, the rice cereal coated bibs, and the walks with the stroller that were a part of our days there. Swinging on the porch swing, I looked with wonderment at our future in our new home, taking a guess at what that future may be, but not knowing. Not really. Caught between two houses—between our past and our future—I was able only to blink back my tears and give thanks for all that had been, and pray for all that would be.

§   §   §

Bless this new home. Keep us safe. Keep us whole. Keep us family.

CHAPTER THIRTY-SEVEN

No, Mama

*M*y children are all telling me "no." Each one of them is doing it somewhat differently, but the effect is the same. Jamilet, who just turned two, often yells the word in mid-air, squirming feverishly as I try to redirect her from some imminent catastrophe—an outlet, a stove knob, a pair of scissors—to a toy—any toy.

Liam, seven, uses a bit more sophistication with his no's. Liam already understands that he should not say no to a parent and has decided to substitute "but" instead.

"Liam, time for bed."

"But I'm not finished with my book."

"Liam, put your socks in their drawer."

"But Jacob didn't put his away."

Jacob, ten, occasionally falls back on Liam's technique, but is moving towards something even more ingenious—the "yes" that means "no."

"Jacob, pick up your school uniform from your bedroom floor."

"Okay." Fifteen minutes later, the uniform is still there.

When I first became a parent, I felt like I had a new under-standing of God. I stared in wonder at newborn Jacob, over-whelmed by my love for him, and marveled that this love I felt for my son was just a sliver of God's love for me.

Now, with the newborn years a cozy memory, my children continue to help me understand God as parent.

God the parent has requests and demands of us, just as I have demands and requests of my children. Sometimes we feel what God is asking of us in the deepness of our being—we hear God's call in our souls. Other times, God speaks to us through scripture—a reading at church, a Bible verse at home. And still other times the Holy Spirit moves through a conver-sation and we sense what God is asking of us.

And while sometimes we say, "yes," right away to what God asks of us, more often we respond like Jamilet, Liam and Jacob. Like toddler Jamilet, we do not always see when we are headed for self-destruction—we think if we can just get to that stove knob, everything will be great. Intent on our own pleasure, we ignore God's warnings and pleas for our safety. Like Liam, we tell God "but." We point out to God that He isn't asking our neighbors to do the same thing. We make excuses for not doing God's will. We try to put God on hold. And finally, perhaps we are most often like ten-year-old Jacob. We hear a reading or homily in church—we know what God is asking of us and at that moment, we say "yes." But then, too quickly, we forget what we agreed to do.

While I understand that my children's "no's" are all devel-opmentally appropriate, I also know that for our family to function effectively and for my children to learn responsibility, I need to teach them to say "yes."

I have to make Jamilet realize that when I say "no" and she does not stop, she will be physically lifted away from the danger. Liam needs to know that no matter how many "buts" he comes up with, the end result will be the same—he will need to do as I asked. And Jacob needs to understand that if he does not put the clothes away the first time, he will still need to do so 15 minutes later, and by then I probably will have added another job.

My experience is that God operates similarly. When we ignore God or tell God "no," God the parent does not back off. Instead, God continues to call us to what would be best for us or for the greater world. Just as my children do not always understand why they need to go to bed, stop playing with the scissors or help keep the house neat, we, as adults do not always fully appreciate where God is leading us. Too often, because we cannot see the bigger picture of where our life fits into God's plan, we choose not to summon the courage to trust God's vision over our own.

But when we do summon that courage to trust; when we do say "yes" to God's call; it is then that we begin to glimpse the bigger picture. We start to see where it is we fit. And we begin to understand that everything God asks of us is within our capabilities.

My plan is that someday, I will not even need to ask Jacob to pick up his uniform from the floor. He will do it on his own. On that day (and I hope it's coming soon), Jacob and I will have a shared vision of a bedroom without crumpled clothes on the floor. Someday, Liam will notice on his own that he is tired and should go to bed. And someday, Jamilet will realize that I really do have her best interest in mind when I don't let her play with the knives.

I do not know when that day is that my children will see the bigger picture—when their "yes" to me will come before I even make the request. Right now, it is enough for me that I see progress. Liam, after all, no longer lunges for the stove knobs like his little sister. And despite Jacob's struggles with the clothes on the floor, he has become very good at going to bed with just one reminder. Everyone is moving forward, and as a parent, that is all I am asking for. Hopefully, God sees the same progress in us.

❧　❧　❧

Forgive me, Lord, for all my no's.
Give me the courage to say "Yes" to You.

CHAPTER THIRTY-EIGHT

Summertime Parenting

*P*arenting in the summer is an entirely different job than it is in any other season. I do not know if this is true in places like Florida or California, where it is warm all year round, but parenting for the 90 days (if you're lucky) of Wisconsin summer is one of the sweetest jobs there is.

First of all, I love the smell of sunscreen. Each morning, I lather it liberally on my three children. They each have a different feel. Jacob is bony and lean. I can count his ribs underneath my fingers as I rub the sunscreen into his back and his chest. Liam seems to be hyper-sensitive to either the coolness of the sunscreen or to my touch and often wiggles his way across the room as I am applying. Jamie has darker skin than the two boys, and probably does not need quite as much sunscreen because of this, but wants twice as much. Her soft, baby skin is such a pleasure to touch, I often give her a second coat, just to make us both happy.

I love the freedom of summer clothes. In the winter, just getting the entire family out the door takes 15 or 20 minutes of preparation. Mittens need to be found, boots are still wet from the day before, then there is the daily debate about the necessity of hats and scarves. In summer, even shoes are optional.

Kids are made for outdoor life, and the summer accommodates them so well. In the summer, you can eat outside, where it doesn't matter if you drip or spill. Food is simpler in the summer. Eight-ingredient casseroles are replaced by hot dogs on the grill.

Toddlers, especially, are summer creatures. A hose, a plastic wading pool and a few beach toys will keep Jamie occupied and in one place longer than any of her indoor toys. Summer recreation is also more toddler-friendly. This past winter, the older boys could ski, sled and ice skate, but Jamie was too young. Often, Bill and I would split up, with one parent taking the boys on an outing and the other staying home with Jamie. But in the summer, water parks have sections for big and little kids. Lakes offer their built-in "shallow end," and picnics and camping are enjoyed by everyone.

Maybe the most significant thing about the summer is that I seem to appreciate my children more than I do any other time of year. Sitting on the beach as they build sandcastles or play in the water, I have nothing else to do besides watch them. Whether on vacation or just on a little outing, I see them more than I do during the rest of the year. Summer also means the kids are between grade levels. This "between-ness" makes me think more about where they have come from and where they are going. While of course Jacob was in fourth grade all year, I am now somehow amazed he is going into fifth. Each year, the summer months startle me with the reminder that growth is constant. The kids' birthdays are quick, one-day events that involve lots of work, and often, in my rush to get everything ready, I don't often have time to reflect on the milestone of the day itself. The long weeks of summer give me a chance to think about Liam, finished with first grade, going into second, and Jacob really moving up into big-kid land. Unencumbered by lunches to make, homework to check, uniforms to wash and endless school meetings, we are better able to be a family. It is during the summer that I am best able to drink in my children—to simply be with them.

At Mass on the last day of school, the priest mentioned that the only difference between recreate and re-create was the hyphen. He reminded us that our summertime recreation should serve also to re-create us.

For me, summer re-creates our family—an annual sunny, sandy, bright re-creation that I am so thankful for.

⚘   ⚘   ⚘

Loving God, for warmth and sun, I give thanks.
Re-create us in your image.

CHAPTER THIRTY-NINE

Too Much Stuff

There is a Bernstein Bears children's book called *Too Much Stuff*. In the book, Mama Bear looks around the house and decides the family needs to give away many of their things to the needy. Papa bear has fishing supplies he hasn't used in years. Brother Bear and Sister Bear have more games than they could ever play with. And Mama Bear herself admits there is no need to save stacks of magazines and scraps of material from her sewing projects.

We recently moved, and I have been feeling a lot like Mama Bear. Our family has too much stuff. It took six adults nearly five hours to move boxes and boxes of our things to our new house. Then, the following weekend, four young, strong professional movers spent another couple of hours moving our furniture. After that, Bill and I still needed to return to the old house for about four or five carloads of "just what's left in the garage."

I am not completely sure what all this stuff is or where we got it. I doubt that we need more than half of it.

"Live simply so that others may simply live," said St. Elizabeth Ann Seton. Mama Bear would have very much agreed with this. All over the world, there are families who struggle just to put together enough rice and beans for one meal. Our family has so much food that packing the pantry of dry goods to move from house to house took several large boxes. In our own city, there are families who would look at the dressers filled with clothes and boxes of shoes we were moving and assume we must have eight or nine kids, not three. We have enough toys to open our own daycare center, enough paper, pens, markers and art supplies to operate a small school, and enough books to keep every kid in the neighborhood busy reading for the rest of the summer.

In my early twenties, Elizabeth Ann Seton's "Live simply," philosophy was mine as well. I lived in community for a year. Fifteen young adults, we worked in Chicago's central city, serving the poor and came home each night to a converted convent where we each had our own tiny room. We shared all other living quarters. I remember in-depth discussions of whether buying a package of cookies was in keeping with the simple life. When I left my year of service work, I fit all my belongings in my parents' car, with both of my parents and my sister also in the car. What has happened to me?

Family life happened. It used to be all I needed to go running was a pair of running shoes. Now, I need a running stroller for the baby and bikes for each of the boys so that everyone can join in. Every age of childhood seems to come with its own equipment, and since there is an eight-year gap between two-year-old Jamie and ten-year-old Jacob, it means we have both baby-toting equipment and big-kid sports equipment in the garage and basement.

Birthdays, Christmas, Easter, Baptisms and First Communions bring a rush of presents from well-meaning relatives buying more stuff for us. And I cannot blame it all on the kids. As Bill and I have moved from the "Early Marriage" style of decorating (think futons and framed posters) to having specific tastes, we have accumulated quite a bit on our own. And living as a family, rather than in community necessitates a certain amount of material things—from having enough plates so as to be able to invite people over, to owning power tools so that we can fix the house on our own.

So what is the answer? In the Bernstein Bears, the Bear family, under Mama's direction, gives away much of their excess stuff to the needy. Everyone grumbles a bit, but they feel good in the end. In our family, the move has taught me to question our possessions. We had the St. Vincent De Paul Society make one pick-up at our old house and two at our new, so far. I am now less likely to hold onto something thinking we might find a use for it. If we have not used it or worn it in six months, it is better to go to someone who has a more pressing need. Picturing myself packing, moving and unpacking the item gives me an immediate sense of whether or not the item is all that important.

Almost three weeks into life at our new house, we still are not completely unpacked. Yet, the kids play with toys, we eat three meals a day, wear clothes, and use a pretty operable office. The unopened boxes speak directly to the question of too much stuff, as we certainly are not missing what is in those boxes. I want to simplify, but do not have all the answers yet. I am praying to St. Elizabeth Ann Seton for guidance. And maybe I will read that Bernstein Bears book one more time.

❦ ❦ ❦

Loving God, please help us as we struggle
not to be possessed by our possessions.

CHAPTER FORTY

Garden of Eden

*I*t was an unseasonably warm fall day and two-year-old Jamie and I were in the backyard, playing. I had turned the hose on so that she could water some flowers, but Jamie had other ideas—she quickly found our little plastic wading pool left over from the summer and began filling it up. When she had a few inches of water in the wading pool, she wriggled out of her sundress, whipped off her diaper, climbed in and sat down. I considered running into the house to get her swimsuit, but decided against it. Knowing the attention span of a two-year-old, I suspected I would no more get her swimsuit on than she would be finished with the pool and onto something else. So I sat down and watched my naked daughter splash around happily in her outdoor bathtub.

As Jamie played, it struck me as to how completely unselfconscious she was. Every so often, she would get out of the pool and run over to the garage or another part of the yard to get another toy. Sometimes, on her way back to the pool, she would stop to drive her little kiddie car around the patio a few times. It did not occur to her that there was anything unusual about this, that there was anything to be embarrassed of. And as I watched my daughter, I felt wistful. For a flash of a second, I felt as God might have, watching Eve in the garden of Eden—hoping it could last forever. It's not that I didn't want my daughter to someday have appropriate modesty for her private body parts. It's just that I knew that soon after children are old enough to realize some body parts are private, they begin to gauge their own bodies against what they see as an ideal. Girls especially begin to find fault with their bodies.

My daughter, who is so comfortable in her own skin right now, may someday feel that her skin is the wrong color. Someday, she may compare her legs or belly to someone else's and find her own lacking. While now, she is no more conscious of her tush than her toes, someday, she may put a dress or a swimsuit back on a rack because she does not like how it makes her behind look. Even though my plans for my daughter include helping her see herself as beautiful and complete, I know that that it will be hard to compete against magazines filled with beautiful models and a culture that has a very limited vision of what female beauty can be.

One of my favorite school Masses last year included my son's first grade class singing a song that had this line: *Don't let anyone ever tell you that you're anything less than beautiful; don't let anyone ever tell you that you're less than whole.*

The song made me cry, and as I looked around, I noticed the other first-grade moms around me were tearing up as well. I think our tears came because all of us, at some time, had been made to feel less than beautiful. To hear our children sing those words, was to hope, for a moment at least, that our children might escape that feeling, that hurt. The chorus gave voice to the unspoken hope of every mother that her child would always be seen as precious.

I cannot help but think that part of my job for my little daughter is to keep her living in her Garden of Eden as long as I can. I have to believe that every year of early childhood that she feels positively about her body is one more year to fall back on when she is an anxious pre-teen. I plan to tend to her little Garden of Eden by limiting her TV, by not bringing fashion magazines into the house, by not buying into the little girl make-up sets and telling Barbie and her friends to come back when they have more normal proportions. I don't know if all this will work. I am hoping that if I couple it with giving my daughter a taste of outdoor life and sports—and a sample of dance and drama, that she will discover that bodies are for work and for play. And maybe, when she is in first grade, her teacher will have her class sing that song: *Don't let anyone ever tell you that you're anything less than beautiful; don't let anyone ever tell you that you're less than whole.*

My beautiful daughter. I pray she will always feel whole.

❧   ❧   ❧

Loving God, bless this daughter of mine.
May she always see her own beauty.

CHAPTER FORTY-ONE

Joyful, Joyful?

We have come rather late to music lessons. I am not a musical person myself, and while my husband had years of piano lessons, I am the one who generally scans the recreation department booklet for summer and after-school activities, signs the kids up and carts them to and fro. With soccer, baseball, swim lessons and an endless parade of birthday parties, I thought our plate was full enough, and I did not pursue music. It was not even a conscious choice. It was an idea that fell off my radar. (And if truth be told, after it fell off, it was probably run over by the minivan as I backed out of the driveway to yet one more sports practice.)

Last summer, though, we moved in across the street from Hy Pitt, a retired man with a gregarious personality and strong opinions.

"Your children should be taking piano lessons," he told me one day.

I told him if he could work it out for me that I would not have to drive them one more place, I would be happy to sign them up.

So it came to be that Jacob and Liam are receiving weekly piano lessons from 80-something Hy Pitt. Shortly after the boys started their lessons, Bill's parents decided their piano would get more use at our house than at theirs.

So now we have two boys who have each had approximately 30 piano lessons. And the theme of our home is Beethoven's "Joyful, Joyful, We Adore Thee."

A relatively easy melody, "Joyful, Joyful" is the first song Jacob received from Hy that he had actually heard before. Hy uses either his or his children's old piano songbooks to teach the boys, which means easy children's songs popular in the fifties, when his children were young, or in the twenties, when he was young. Either way, our boys had never heard of the songs they were playing until "Joyful, Joyful." Liam is not quite up to the "Joyful, Joyful," level yet, and is still playing songs about random ducks or "crunchy flakes." A child of the 70s, I have never heard of them, either.

The strange thing about Jacob's piano habits, though, is he never sits down for a half-hour of practice. Instead, he grabs a few minutes here or there, and pounds out "Joyful, Joyful." Often, he chooses to practice just as we are about to leave for an activity. Faster at finding and tying his shoes than his little brother and sister, he is ready to go a couple minutes before them. Transition times are not Jamie and Liam's best periods of the day, so the scene becomes a strange mix of screaming and fussing to classical music.

Joyful, joyful, we adore thee.

"Liam, get your shoes on now!"

God of mercy, Lord of love.

"I can't find them. They're gone. Oh, Jamie has one! Give that back!"

Hearts unfold like flowers before thee.

"Jamie, give Liam his shoe, please."

"NO!"

Opening to their sun, above.

Eventually, all shoes are on the correct children, and "Joyful" is abandoned as we rush out the door.

Later in the day, Jacob will hit the piano again—at a different transition time—say, Jamie and Liam's bedtime, which is forty-five minutes earlier than his. For whatever reason, my mind always picks up on the line he left off on last time he played. I guess this is helpful, as it provides a different background for the fussing.

Melt the clouds of sin and sadness.

"She walked into the bathroom WITHOUT KNOCKING!"

Drive the dark of doubt away.

"My toothbrush!"

Giver of immortal gladness

"No, that is MINE. I don't want YOUR GERMS!"

Fill us with the light of day.

Sometimes, I notice that if Jamie and Liam's argument escalates, Jacob plays faster. It is all Bill and I can do to get the two younger ones in bed before they are launched into orbit by sheer emotion, and I worry that Jacob could actually break the piano by playing too hard and too fast.

But every so often, when all things align, Liam and Jamie have a transitional moment that gives me a glimpse of hope. Jacob's playing slows, becomes beautiful, and I am so thankful that when I backed over the potential for music lessons, I did not crush them completely.

Thou art giving

"Goodnight, Jamie. Can I have a hug?"

And forgiving.

"I love you, Liam."

Ever blessing

"I love you, too."

Ever blest.

Ever blessed, indeed. Not because things are always joyful, joyful. But because every once in awhile, hearts do unfold.

❧   ❧   ❧

Loving God, help my children to learn to find joy in each other.

CHAPTER FORTY-TWO

Cleaning the Kitchen

I would be a much more spiritual person if I did not need to clean the kitchen.

We belong to two parishes, and both these parishes offer excellent adult education programs on matters of faith. Both offer various types of prayer groups. Sometimes the programs are in the evenings, other times they are on weekends. They are offered in all the church seasons of the year.

And Bill and I hardly go to anything.

We have not always been like this. In college, I went to just about every spiritual or social justice program Marquette University offered. As young adults, Bill and I attended Theology on Tap religiously. We stayed after church for the Advent and Lenten series. We joined the home-based discussion groups. We were involved in our church.

Now, we go to church on Sunday, and I am very active in the kids' school, but we no longer do much in terms of our own continuing spiritual education. And I am blaming the kitchen. Okay, not just the kitchen. I will also blame the laundry and the sticky floor and the school papers. And I am blaming the kitchen and laundry and the floor because I don't want to blame the children.

The truth is that each successive child has made it that much harder to leave for an evening or weekend afternoon. It is not just a babysitting issue—although that is part of it. A bigger problem for me is children make everything take longer. When Bill and I were first married, we could clean up the kitchen after dinner in 10 or 15 minutes. Six o'clock dinner, with a seven o'clock program at church? No problem. There were only two plates to clean and a pot to scrub. The floor didn't even need sweeping. We had two adults to do this tiny bit of work, uninterrupted. That same job, eleven years and three children later, takes three to four times as long. Not only are there more dishes, there is one fewer adult to do the work, as someone needs to restrain the two-year-old from "helping" too much. The parent left to clean, while having the help of the seven and ten-year-old, is simultaneously cleaning, teaching young boys to clean, and often re-cleaning after the young boys. The floor that did not need sweeping after the two-adult dinner, sometimes needs a bulldozer after the two-adult, three-kid dinner. And after spaghetti, the walls near the high chair need to be wiped down or repainted.

The kitchen cleaning example can be multiplied by every chore in the house—there is more laundry, more toys to pick up, more papers to sort—and less time to do everything. And I am not a person who needs a dust-free, bookshelf alphabetized environment—anyone who has seen my home knows I am far from being a perfectionist. I don't go to church programs not because I am afraid of imperfection in my home—it is because I am afraid an hour or two away from it will tilt us into chaos.

And yet, even as I write this, glancing across the hall at the boys' room, where their drawer is so jammed full of unfolded underwear, it won't even close, I know I am talking about something that is and is not an excuse at the same time.

This past Advent, after feeding the family frozen pizza for dinner one night, I actually made it to a women's night of reflection at church. As I eased myself into the chair, I mentioned to the woman next to me, also a mother, that I was able to "extract myself from my life," and make it to the program. She nodded in recognition.

Jesus made it pretty clear that one of the requirements of discipleship is a willingness to extract ourselves from our lives. He asked Peter to put down his net and follow him. He told Martha to stop worrying so much about preparing the meal, and sit down and talk with him. Jesus expected different things of both of these people, and I think he bases his expectations partly on where they were in their lives. I am aware that at this point in my life, God is not asking me to completely stop my work and go to a meaningful church program each evening. God is the one, after all, who saw fit to lend me these three children to look after during my stay here—and that includes the spaghetti flinger.

But I think God is asking me to do more than I am doing. Bill and I have both noticed that while we had more time to give to spirituality in our twenties, a little time of grace and reflection goes a longer way now that we are in our thirties. It is almost as if God recognizes that we have so little free time and rushes to meet us where we are. Jesus, in fact, wasn't asking Martha to stop working for the rest of her life—but rather just to give him a little time for that evening.

For me, the challenge is in recognizing when Jesus is at my

door—in hearing him tell me to put down my work. The challenge is finding a balance between entering into the pace of life with three children, and extracting myself from that life. The challenge is giving God that opportunity to rush to meet me.

❧   ❧   ❧

Loving God, I have just a moment.
Be with me in this moment. Rush to me.

CHAPTER FORTY-THREE

The Gap

*T*his past weekend, my husband and I went to a party where we knew the hosts but almost no one else. As we mingled and met people at the party, I was asked a few times how many children we had and what their ages were.

"Two boys and a girl," I would answer. "Ten, seven and two."

The conversations rolled on, but I had a hard time getting past that simple question.

Sometimes, the five-year age gap between seven-year-old Liam and two-year-old Jamilet looms large. We had two foster children in that gap before Jamilet joined our family. Tonisha is four years old now, and part of me thinks she belongs in my gap.

How old are your children?

Ten, seven, four and two.

It looks neater to me. It makes more sense. One baby every two or three years. Four all together.

I know the five-year gap between Liam and Jamilet probably feels as big as it ever will. Jamilet is still more baby than little girl, and Liam has just entered the big-kid world of soccer practice and chapter books. Five years might as well be a generation when it is the difference between Teletubbies and Batman.

And that is where the four-year-old would come in. Four-year-old Tonisha would be able to go up or down. She could kick the soccer ball around with Liam, and also be happy playing blocks with Jamilet. She would bridge that gap. Jamilet is in a car seat. Liam has graduated into the regular seat of the car. Tonisha would be in a booster, right in the middle.

I realize that with the ability to play up with Liam, or down with Jamilet, Tonisha would also bring more sibling conflict into the family. Able to play with either, she would get into skirmishes with both. Even in my imagination, while the spacing is perfect, the children are not.

Maybe what also bothers me about that five-year gap is the lack of symmetry I sometimes feel in the family. I have a partner in Bill. Jacob and Liam have each other. And while, of course, Jamilet has all of us, she does not have someone who lines up with her. She is the only one in our family with her own room. Tonisha could share her room.

But Tonisha has been gone over a year. There is no reason to think she is coming back. Yet, still she dances in my mind. Her giggle is what comes between Liam and Jamilet. Tonisha left our family, and in her place we have a span of sixty months between our second and third children. To me, that span will always be Tonisha's place. A place she is always welcome to come back to, should she ever need it. A place she could reclaim in a heartbeat.

She lived with us for over a year, and in that time, she made us a better family. She expanded our notion of love—showing us how strangers become family. Her smile was testament to the resiliency of the human spirit, even as her case notes spoke to the fragility of family life. With limited details of her past, and social service's uncertain plan for her future, Tonisha forced us to live in the present. She taught us that family is about who is here right now—not who was here before and who might come later. Maybe most importantly, Tonisha taught us that the hurt that comes after loving and then letting go is survivable. She helped us learn that the pushes on the swing and the Frisbee tosses and the fuzzy footed pajamas outweigh that very heavy moment of goodbye.

And because of all these things, her echo remains. Part of Tonisha's echo is a five-year gap that shows that life is not always neat; not always symmetrical.

Tonisha's echo is a gap that makes me pause at a party when I am asked a very simple question.

How many children do you have?

℘   ℘   ℘

Loving God, I give you the gaps in my life.
The questions that may never be answered.

CHAPTER FORTY-FOUR

Giving Thanks for Nothing

I had 12 bags of groceries to unload from the car. Thanksgiving was two days away and we were hosting dinner for 22. As I carried the first bags into the house, I looked at the toys everywhere, the laundry to sort, the pile of mail and school papers on the kitchen table. I decided it would take every free hour from that moment until Thanksgiving just to get the house in presentable shape and the food cooked and ready.

Bag by bag, I brought the groceries in. Two-year-old Jamilet stood next to the car in the driveway and watched me walk through the garage and into the house making the trips.

"Pretzels," she said, watching me grab a bag. "Yogurt. Bread. Lunchtime?"

I told her it would be lunchtime right after I brought in all the groceries, and went into the house. One more bag to go. I left her leaning casually against the car door.

"Time for lunch," I said to Jamilet, when I came back to the car. I looked down at her. She was holding an empty bottle of prescription allergy pills, the cap in one hand, the bottle in the other. Where had she gotten that? I felt alarm rising within me.

"Where did you get that bottle?"

"Bottle in car."

"Open your mouth." I swept her mouth with my fingers. There were no pills in her mouth, but just inside her lip was a white powdery substance. I swallowed.

"Did you eat the pills?"

"Empty," she said.

I wanted to believe her. I grabbed the bottle, carried her in and called Poison Control.

"How many did she eat?" the woman on the other end asked me.

"I'm not sure she ate any," I said. "The bottle might have been empty. I'm not even sure why the bottle was in the car."

"Is it possible she ate ten pills?" the woman asked.

"It's possible. I just don't know. She was alone for about a minute."

"For her weight, ten pills is lethal. You need to take her to the nearest emergency room. I'll call ahead so they know you're coming."

I looked at Jamilet.

"Did you eat these?" I asked, again.

"Empty," she said.

Empty. I strapped her into her car seat. She was probably right, but ten pills were lethal and where had the powdery residue in her mouth come from?

At the emergency room, they took her temperature and pulse. All were normal, but it suddenly became obvious to me just how serious the situation could become. The nurse on duty said the toxic dose for Jamilet's weight was really more like five pills than ten. I called Bill, and he left work and sped over. Jamilet stuck by her story as Bill, a doctor, then two nurses, came in to ask her if she ate some pills. The final nurse even tried to lead her into saying she ate the pills.

"This bottle is empty because you ate the pills up, isn't it?" the nurse said, smiling. "Were they yummy?"

"Empty," Jamilet said.

Still, as a precaution, the E.R. staff said she should be hooked up to an E.K.G. and be observed for six hours—the amount of time it could take the drugs to activate in her system.

As they put the stickers with wires all over my baby's chest and back, the nurse said she would bring in some charcoal for Jamilet to drink. Just in case, she said. The charcoal would absorb the medicine. I blinked back my tears. I was so sorry I had left her alone. Sorry that Bill or I had been careless enough to leave an allergy bottle—even an empty one—in the car. Sorry that I was putting her through six hours of observation when she had trouble sitting still for a ten-minute book. And to be honest, I was a little sorry for myself, too. With no time to spare before Thanksgiving, I would be spending the next six hours in the E.R. with a child who was possibly not sick at all.

An hour went by, with Jamilet sitting quietly on my lap, unusually calm, hooked up to the E.K.G. She cooperatively drank the charcoal drink they gave her, flavored, the nurse said, with six tablespoons of chocolate sauce. After an hour and a half with no change, I was even more convinced she had not eaten any pills. She fell asleep on my chest, and I eased my way back into the bed, and pulled my feet up. For two hours, she slept—her usual nap time. Not wanting to wake her with the TV, I simply lay in bed and listened to her breathing. She was warm against my body, and looked smaller than usual in her tiny hospital gown. Normally, during Jamilet's nap, I rush to get a hundred things done—phone interviews for articles, writing, editing, cleaning. And now it was nap time and she was asleep on my chest in a hospital. Bill was grading eighth grade essays on a chair nearby.

As she slept, it occurred to me that she and I had never done this before. I had cradled newborn Jacob and Liam in my arms and held them in wonder as they slept in the hospital after they were born. Jamilet and I had never had that time. She came to us at age 13 months as a foster child, already a good napper and sleeper. There had never been a reason to hold her as she slept. But now there was.

As she slept, I rubbed her skin, that unbelievably soft baby skin. Trapped in an E.R. room, two days before Thanksgiving, I understood that this was my time to experience newborn Jamilet.

And so I did. I let go of all the things I had to do, and gave thanks for the emergency that was not. I marveled at my sleeping daughter. I fingered her curls, and gently touched her lips. I watched her heartbeat on the monitor as I felt it against my chest. I prayed for her—thanking God for the gift of her life. Thanking God that our afternoon at the hospital was all for nothing. For nothing at all.

§   §   §

Loving God, I thank you for averted tragedies,
for the accidents that never happened,
for the health we take for granted.

CHAPTER FORTY-FIVE

Frozen Boys

My boys were playing freeze tag with some friends the other night and having finished the dinner dishes, I sat on the front porch and watched. Liam had only played the game a couple times before, and was taking the rule about being frozen very seriously. While Jacob would stop and casually stand in one place when tagged, Liam held the exact position he had been in at the time of the tag. I watched with amusement as Liam struggled to balance on one foot, arms extended, not even blinking, until someone ran by to unfreeze him again.

If I could, I would freeze the current ages of my two boys for a couple of extra years. At seven and ten, they are full-throttle in the middle of childhood, and it is my favorite stage so far. Their three-year age difference, which seemed like quite a gap when they were younger, has finally narrowed. They can play together well, and Jacob is kind enough to go easy on his little brother to keep Liam's frustration at bay. They no longer need the constant supervision their sister requires. A nice mix of dependence and independence, they are old enough to put their own pajamas on, but young enough to still want to be tucked in.

Maybe it is the former junior high teacher in me that wants to gently tap each of my boys and tell them they are frozen at seven and ten. I know about the attitudes that can come when kids turn 12 or 13, and I am enjoying the absence of eye-rolling and talking back while I still can.

As far as I can tell, our boys are holding onto their child-hood a little longer than some of their peers. Bill and I have limited their exposure to TV, movies and even popular songs. It has left them a little out of sync with pop culture, but I think it has also kept them innocent longer. With no cable, no Game Boy, Game Cube and i-Pod, there is nothing for them to do but play and read. Nothing to do but be a kid.

But while I can keep them from growing up before their time, I cannot freeze them in mid-childhood forever any more than I can hurry their sister through the unreasonable two's and toward the more rational three-year-old stage. I cannot freeze them any more than I can freeze my own age. Time dic-tates its own pace.

What I am hoping, though, is that I can learn from my cur-rent desire to hold onto the present. So often, as a parent, I have looked ahead or behind. When the boys were babies, I longed for the time when I could sleep through the night. When they started school, I looked back wistfully to our lazy mornings cuddling together. Now, rooted in the present, I am (finally) appreciating them for the age they are. Fully enjoying my boys at their current age makes me wonder if what I am looking for is not a forever seven- and ten-year-old, but rather, a spirit of enjoyment and wonder for my children, no matter what their age. Maybe I am looking for the grace to see the beauty in every age—even those ages that might seem more difficult, like two or thirteen.

I will pray that God will give me the grace to enjoy my children when they are teens just as much as I enjoy them right now. And who knows, maybe when Jacob is 16 and Liam is 13, I will say it doesn't get any better than this, only to be proven wrong again when they are 24 and 21. I don't know. I do know though, that seven and ten is wonderful. Scooters and soccer. Freeze tag and kickball. Popsicles and chapter books. I can't freeze it, but I can savor it. I can drink it in. And I am. I certainly am.

ॐ   ॐ   ॐ

Loving God, I feel your presence in the wonder of my children. Thank you. Thank you.

CHAPTER FORTY-SIX

Holy Silence

*T*his past Sunday, two-year-old Jamie seemed especially calm during Mass. I don't know if it was the Superman fruit snacks I brought along or her newfound ability to draw circles, but I found myself able to attend to the liturgy in a way I haven't in awhile. And, very oddly for me, what jumped out was the Psalm response.

I know I am not supposed to play favorites with parts of the Mass, but I do. I most look forward to the homily and a good one will stick with me for a week or more. My husband and I still talk about several excellent homilies that are now years in the past. Besides the homily, the Eucharist, the Gospel, the Sign of Peace, the second reading and songs—probably in that order—tend to speak to me the most at Mass. Too often, I regard the first reading, Psalm response, and various other beautiful prayers as transitional parts of the Mass that propel me toward my more favorite parts. Most Sundays, if you would ask me what the Psalm was, I would stare at you blankly. But this past Sunday, Psalm 137 leapt out at me. "Let my tongue be silent, O Lord my God, if I should ever forget about you."

To me, that Psalm is laden with meaning, on so many levels.

The first thing that came to mind as I sang the words was the difference between my husband and me. Bill is a quiet person. While not shy, he will never be the one to dominate a conversation or a meeting. I have never heard him interrupt someone he was speaking to. He is careful about what he says and what he does not say. "You rarely get in trouble for what you don't say," he observed once. "The more you talk, the more likely you're going to say something you regret."

I, on the other hand, am a talker. I will talk anywhere, and with anyone. I hope I am a good listener, too, but I know no one would describe me as quiet. I love the spoken word just as I love the written word. I have yet to meet a form of communication I don't like. E-mail, phone calls, letters, cards, talking while doing sports or doing dishes, chatting at a bar or at a church potluck. I love it all. And perhaps that is why this Psalm struck me so. "Let my tongue be silent O Lord, my God, if I should ever forget about you." In those words is an admonition for those of us who have the gift of the gab: be careful what you talk about.

I once read that there are three levels of conversation — the lowest level is having a conversation about things, the middle level is having a conversation about people and the highest form of communication is talking about ideas. The Psalm reminds us that if a spirit of the holy does not underline that which we talk about, we have no business chatting at all. This does not mean that we must always speak of lofty ideas — much of life involves talking about when the brake pads should be changed — but our conversation should not lead us away from what is good.

The other reason the Psalm struck me was because of something I have been saying to my boys lately. I have little patience for them being critical of each other, tattling on each other or complaining about what I made for dinner. My catch phrase as

of late has been, "If it's not positive or neutral, don't say it at all."
After explaining what neutral meant to Liam, I have had a lot of
success with this phrase. I use it to cut off conversations before
they even begin. A boy glances at his broccoli with a look of
horror. "If it's not positive or neutral, don't say it," I will tell him,
taking a bite of my own broccoli. When one of them comes in
from outside with a look of rage because of a foul on the basket-
ball court or a bad pass in football, I use the phrase before he
can say anything. "If it's not positive or neutral. . ."

The phrase doesn't always work, but I have found it cuts
down on negative comments. Hearing the Psalmist say the same
thing to ancient Israel that I say in my kitchen is reassuring to
me as a parent. My advice for my boys is thousands of years old.
It is so sage that it is in the Bible. Maybe not the exact words,
but the idea.

Finally, the Psalm strikes me as a perfect beginning to any
meeting. Most meetings I go to (other than those at work) begin
with prayer. To say, "Let my tongue be silent O Lord my God, if
I should ever forget about you," is the most powerful way to
begin a meeting that I can think of. It is a prayer that invites God
to help us speak, and it is a prayer for the courage to be silent.

As a talker, married to a quiet guy, with two talkers and one
quiet guy as children, I am holding onto this phrase. I think it
speaks to all five of us. The quiet among us understand its wisdom
intuitively. We chatters need more reminders. "Let my tongue be
silent O Lord, my God, if I should ever forget about you."

ॐ   ॐ   ॐ

Loving God, be the inspiration behind my words.

CHAPTER FORTY-SEVEN

Startling Growth

*A*ll the trees outside my window have leaves today. Full leaves, not just buds. I sit at this desk every day, but last time I remember looking out the window, the trees had only the tiniest buds. I remember thinking that spring comes so late to Wisconsin. I remember staring out the window, between paragraphs, wondering when the leaves would arrive. And then today, I look out, and boom — leafy trees. Green everywhere. Looking out the window, I am so happy to see the greenness and the bright pink of the crabapple tree, but I wonder when it happened. I know the buds did not become leaves overnight. Why didn't I take note as the buds grew? Did I go weeks without looking out the window or did I look without seeing? Why do the leaves appearing seem sudden to me, instead of gradual, as I know was the reality?

I fear the same thing is happening to my children. Jamie goes on the potty now. Her diaper pail has been empty for how long? Two weeks? Three? I honestly don't know. One day she said she wanted to go on the potty, and each day after that, she stayed dry longer and longer. I bought her some underwear, knowing full well that she could be back in diapers the next day, but she wasn't. She potty trained herself—my first child to do this. I had nothing to do with it, and because of that, I cannot say when it happened, exactly. I will probably never buy a pack of diapers again, until I buy them for our grandchildren. Yet, at the time I bought my last pack of diapers, I had no idea it would be my last. It wasn't even the biggest size.

Liam is reading Harry Potter books. Wasn't he just reading those Magic Treehouse easy chapter books last month? Or was it the month before? Where did Harry Potter come from? I guess, if I really thought about it, I would admit that I saw some Beverly Clearys in between the easy chapter books and the 300-page Harry Potter. But it still feels sudden. My little Liam, curled up on the couch with such a big book.

Jacob is in contacts. He has never worn glasses, but we took him to the eye doctor and it turned out he needed corrected vision. Apparently, age 11 is old enough for contacts. So now, as the kids get ready in the morning, I walk past the bathroom to see Jacob, index finger to his eye, putting in his contacts. Wasn't I just brushing his teeth for him last week? It was not last week, I remind myself. It was when he was three. But sometimes that feels like last week. And now he wears contacts.

Growth is such a strange thing to witness as a parent. I eagerly await a stage of childhood to end so that my child is bigger and more capable, but then when it does finally end, I look back wistfully at what used to be. I look at picture albums from two years past and am amazed at how young my children look.

I am still learning how to appreciate the moment—to really live in the moment as a parent and experience who my children are right now. It is the only way I know of to slow down time.

Once, when I was about eleven, school was canceled because of a snow day. The snow was so deep and drifted so high that no cars could pass in front of our house. I pulled on my jacket and snow pants, and went out in the early morning, before anyone had a chance to disturb the snow. I lay in a drift in the front of our house and looked up at the sky. I had never heard it so silent outside before. As I lay there, I thought to myself, "I will never forget this. I will never forget how the sky looks and how quiet it is." I was completely present to the cold air, the gray sky, and the soft snow. I experienced a peace that I had not known before. And I never forgot that moment. That memory of lying outside in the snow is as clear to me today as it was the day after it happened. But it is so difficult to make a conscious decision to remember something—as much as we love our children, it is so hard to be completely present to them and nothing else. Yet without regularly taking time to give them our complete presence, we risk being startled with their growth. We risk having years of their life that are, at best, a hazy memory.

The reason, after all, that I did not see the buds change to leaves outside of my office window is that I was not attentive to the buds. I had other things to do—articles to write, e-mails to send, and bills to pay. These were necessary things, and I don't regret missing watching the buds change in order to do them. I know, too, that there are necessary things to get done as my children grow, and it would not be good for them—or for me—to be focused on my children every second of the day. But amid all the necessary things to get done, there are also some things that can be put aside. There are snowdrift opportunities being offered to me each week. Moments that I could remember for a lifetime, if only I would choose to be present to them, and nothing else. And I pray I may put aside the unnecessary so as to be present to my children. So as not to spend my life wondering how the buds became leaves.

❧ ❧ ❧

Loving God, help me to remember to pause.

CHAPTER FORTY-EIGHT

Blessed?

I love each of my children so much that the thought of losing any one of them can bring on a physical reaction. Last night, a story of a little boy dying in a car accident made the news, and my mind, just for a moment, allowed that child to become my child. Just for a moment, it was Jacob who died in that car accident. The thought was so terrible that my breathing started coming in gulps, and I began to gag. I tried to pull away from the words and images, but my mind paid no heed. It went to that "what if" place that, on most days, I am able to avoid visiting. As I tried to screech my thoughts to a halt, my brain played out the scene, and I was dragged along, a reluctant viewer.

Our children have had a very healthy time of it so far. In my eleven years of parenting, I have picked up prescription medicine for one of the kids a total of just three times. They have missed maybe ten days of school, combined, since our oldest, Jacob, started pre-school, eight years ago. We have had two broken bones so far, and three stitches. I don't know if it is because they are coordinated or are not big risk-takers, but I doubt that we have gone through more than a couple boxes of Band-Aids in the past decade, not counting the ones Jamie wears just because she likes the way they look on her fingers. We are blessed with health, I would say, if the word "blessed" did not stick in my throat.

I don't know why my children are so healthy. While I can feel blessed, I am hesitant to say we are blessed, because it seems to imply that a parent with a seriously ill child isn't so blessed. If God is giving my children their health, what does that say about all the other children who have chronic diseases or get injured—or killed—in accidents?

God created a physical world for us, with physical limitations. Bones can break, organs can fail, cancer cells can divide. Hearts can stop. And while miracles do happen, it seems that more often, the course of an illness or injury is subject to the laws of nature and the limitations of medical science.

My own faith hovers in that middle ground between nature's roll of the dice and "everything happens for a reason." The reason so many children are starving, after all, has nothing to do with God's will for them and everything to do with an unequal distribution of wealth in the world.

Perhaps good health itself is not the blessing. Perhaps the blessing of good health is that it affords us the time and energy to reach out to others.

A good friend has a daughter with Type 1 diabetes. My friend has to spend hours each week managing her daughter's care. She often gets up in the middle of the night to check her daughter's sugar levels. She gives her daughter insulin injections at least four times a day. She is constantly aware of exactly when her daughter needs to eat and exercise, so her sugar levels do not spike too high or dip too low.

None of my children are diabetic, and because of this, I have many hours each week "free" that my friend does not have. It is not enough simply be thankful for my healthy kids and move on. It is not enough to label them blessed.

If, as Jesus told the parents of the blind man, their son's blindness was not God's punishment for his sins or their sins, but rather a way to display the work of God in his life, so too, must parents of healthy children realize their children's health is a way to display the work of God. With less to worry about in our own families, we are called to take that saved time and energy to concern ourselves with those who need us.

Statistics show that the lower an income a family has, the bigger percentage of that income they typically give to charity. So while the very wealthy often give the biggest donations in terms of actual amounts of money, it is the middle class and the poor who give the larger slice of their own family dollars.

I have seen the same too often be true in terms of families struggling with an illness. My friend with the diabetic daughter, for example, will be the first to make a casserole or pot of soup for a household with a new baby or a sick family member.

It is often the doing without—whether it is money or health—that helps us look with empathy toward others also doing without.

So maybe it is when our own road is easiest—when it is difficult to imagine the hardships that some families must go through—that we most need prayer. During these smooth-sailing times, maybe we need to go to God, not to simply give thanks for our blessings, but to ask, "What now? What would you like me to do?"

The answer we receive will be the real blessing.

❧   ❧   ❧

Loving God, guide me to recognize the easy parts of my life
so that I can use my blessings for service.

CHAPTER FORTY-NINE

Final Thoughts

*D*ear Jacob, Liam and Jamilet,

You cannot know how much I love you. How much I think about you. You cannot know how some parts of this world scare me, when I think of what you could encounter in your life. You cannot imagine the joy I wish for you. You cannot know what it is to be a mother — how it feels to somehow be living my own life, yet experiencing three other lives, as well.

You cannot know these things because you are not supposed to know them. Your life belongs to you, not me. I understand this, yet, last night at your baseball game, Jacob, when you hit that ball straight and hard over the second baseman's head, a piece of me ran to first with you. A piece of me stood on the base, safe, and got ready to run to second. And Liam, this morning, when you told me of that terrible dream you had, the dream where there were bombs in the room, I was afraid for you. The dream seemed so real, and you told me about it so seriously, that I was afraid. Your life belongs to you, Jamie, yet, when I look at that picture of our family sitting together on the couch, I see my own smile in your smile. It's so obvious it makes me laugh. We have the same smile.

The crazy thing about being a parent is that, often, it's the time that I am completely alone that I love you the most. When we are all together, I am so busy. I am strapping you into the high chair, Jamie, or reading your spelling words to you, Liam, or signing your tests from school, Jacob. When we are all together, it is all about action and what we're doing at the time. But when I am alone, and you are away or in bed, all that action is gone for the moment. And when the action is gone, I am able to think about who you are, not what you are doing. And it is who you are that I love so deeply.

When I first became a mother, I was fearful that I would become less of who I am. I was afraid that the person I was would be boiled down to an apostrophe 's.' I was afraid that all I would be was Jacob's mom and that the rest of me might just disappear in that. What I discovered, though, was that parenthood pulled me to a place where I am even more of myself. I am indeed an apostrophe 's.' Apostrophe 's' three times over, in fact. But those apostrophes have taught me more about who I am and what I am capable of than any other punctuation mark could have.

Jacob, Liam and Jamie, I pray that throughout your lives, you will always feel the intense love that your dad and I have for you. I pray that this love will be both a ladder and a safety net for you. We stand ready to steady you as you climb higher and catch you if you fall. We love you more than you could ever know.

– Mom

CHAPTER FIFTY

Epilogue

This entire book was written during nap time. I wrote the early chapters while three-year-old Jacob and baby Liam took their afternoon naps. The middle chapters I wrote while Jacob was in kindergarten and toddler Liam snoozed away. Lucinda, then Tonisha joined our family when Liam was in four-year-old kindergarten. They cooperatively picked up the afternoon naps where Liam left off, and I was able to keep writing. Finally, Jamie arrived. The most gifted sleeper of all five, her naps were often an astounding four hours long. Jamie's naps even allowed time for edits and rewrites.

Through most of my eleven years of napping babies, toddlers and preschoolers, I didn't even know I was putting together a book — I was just writing down my experiences of motherhood. As my children slept, I tapped away at my keyboard, capturing a moment of parenting that struck me as important. Many times, the dishes sat unwashed in the sink and the laundry remained unfolded in the basket (if it even made it out of the dryer at all), as I wrote.

Sometimes it seemed that nap time was the highlight of my day. Mornings were ABC blocks, tricycle rides, sticky hands to wipe, and socks to find. Late afternoons meant it was time to get homework started, make dinner, and drive to soccer practice. But sandwiched in between was nap time. Nap time was the only time of the day I was completely alone. As my children slept, I had time to think about what parenting meant beyond the dried Play-Doh that was stuck to the kitchen floor. I had time to think about where God was taking our family. How being a mother was changing me as a person. Nap time was when I took a breath.

I am so thankful for those nap times. Thankful for the stillness and silence. I am thankful for the calm that would wash over me each day as I sat down at my computer—a calm that came from being able to see the bigger picture, if just for a moment.

I once read that children do most of their growing while they are asleep. When I look back over my thousands of nap time words, hundreds of nap time paragraphs, dozens and dozens of nap time pages, I realize that yes, indeed, my children have grown. And we have words to show this growth—infant, toddler, child, pre-teen. But we have no such words to delineate the changes that take place in a mother as her children get older.

I wish we did.

For I am a different mother now than I was during my first nap time.

As my children slept, I grew as well.

❧ ❧ ❧